LIGHT YEARS

Table of Contents

ONE

For all the stalwart lightkeepers, past & present
For all the writers finding their own light to shine
& with & for Jeff, as always

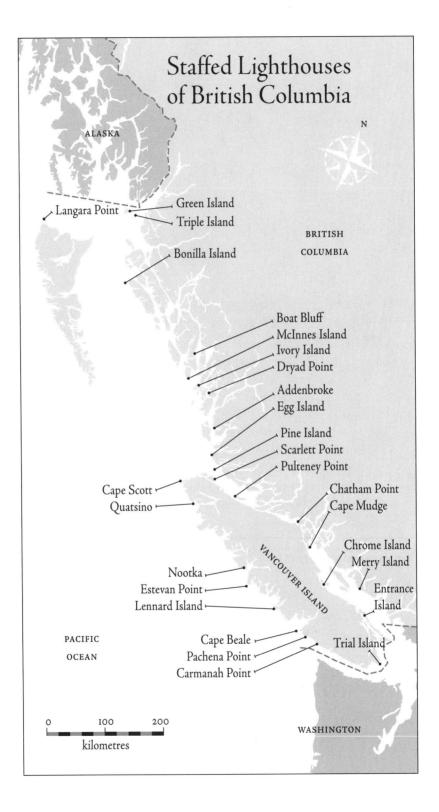

Staffed Lighthouses
of British Columbia

N

ALASKA

Langara Point

Green Island

Triple Island

BRITISH

Bonilla Island

COLUMBIA

Boat Bluff

McInnes Island

Ivory Island

Dryad Point

Addenbroke

Egg Island

Pine Island

Scarlett Point

Pulteney Point

Cape Scott

Chatham Point

Quatsino

Cape Mudge

Chrome Island

Merry Island

Nootka

Estevan Point

VANCOUVER ISLAND

Entrance

Lennard Island

Island

PACIFIC

Cape Beale

Trial Island

OCEAN

Pachena Point

Carmanah Point

0   100   200

kilometres

WASHINGTON

LIGHT YEARS

✦ Memoir of a Modern Lighthouse Keeper ✦

CAROLINE WOODWARD

HARBOUR PUBLISHING

HARBOUR PUBLISHING CO. LTD.
PO Box 219, Madeira Park, BC, VON 2H0
www.harbourpublishing.com

All photographs by Jeff George unless otherwise specified
Edited by Pam Robertson
Text design by Shed Simas
Dust jacket design by Anna Comfort O'Keeffe
Printed and bound in Canada
Printed on FSC-certified 50% PCW recycled stock

Harbour Publishing acknowledges the support of the Canada Council for the Arts, which last year invested $157 million to bring the arts to Canadians throughout the country. We also gratefully acknowledge financial support from the Government of Canada through the Canada Book Fund and from the Province of British Columbia through the BC Arts Council and the Book Publishing Tax Credit.

CATALOGUING DATA AVAILABLE FROM LIBRARY AND ARCHIVES CANADA
ISBN 978-1-55017-727-5 (cloth)
ISBN 978-1-55017-728-2 (ebook)

On Becoming
Lighthouse Keepers

IT ALL STARTED WITH A RUNAWAY JACK RUSSELL TERRIER ON THE OPEN deck of a ferry bound from Port McNeill to Alert Bay, off the north coast of Vancouver Island. I'm very much a dog lover, so I scooped up the grey-muzzled fellow before he came to any harm. I held on to him and scanned the drivers and the foot passengers. Soon enough, an anxious middle-aged man appeared and I knew exactly who he was looking for between the rows of parked trucks and moving cars.

That September day in 2006 was brilliantly sunny, and like ferry passengers on the West Coast often do, the Jack Russell owner and I chose to stand outside on the deck of the boat. I was beside my Chev Tracker, packed to the roofline as usual with plastic tubs and cardboard boxes filled with catalogues and books, a reliable conversation piece. We chatted away and I explained the state of my bookmobile in response to his query. I worked as a publishing sales rep for over thirty Canadian, American and European publishers and I was heading over to the historic fishing village for an appointment with Andrea Sanborn, the coordinator of the U'mista Cultural Centre. I had new First Nations art and history books, as well as seafood cookbooks, to show her. We both admired the excellent exhibits and programs at the centre and agreed that Alert Bay was renowned for its artists, past and present.

Then he said something that changed my life. He said he was on his way to a six-week stint as a relief lightkeeper on neighbouring Malcolm Island, the next ferry stop after Alert Bay on Cormorant Island.

"Wow!" I said, and then went on to say what I've now heard from others at least one hundred times over: "I thought all the lighthouses in BC were shut down."

I was patiently educated on the spot with a brief history of government attempts, during the 1980s and 1990s, to de-staff the lighthouses—a policy that was vehemently opposed by mariners, aviators and several strong allies, most notably MP (and later senator) Pat Carney. It was a political debacle, and twenty-seven BC lighthouses as of that fine fall day were still staffed by human beings, although nearly two dozen were automated before federal decision makers called a halt.

Every year, I sold hundreds of copies of two popular history books, *Lights of the Inside Passage* and *Keepers of the Light* by lightkeeper and historian Donald Graham, to booksellers on the BC coast, but I had never made time for more than a quick skim myself. I made a mental note to correct that situation.

My curiosity was really piqued for another reason, though. "Do you have to be an engineer or a mechanic to be a lightkeeper?" I asked. No, explained my kindred spirit and new lightkeeper friend, who gave me a capsule history of his life as a civil servant—he had risen to become a regional manager in the BC Interior. Then he visited one of his sons, who had found work in Port Hardy at the northern tip of Vancouver Island. My new friend felt an immediate excitement upon arrival and bonded with the wild Pacific Ocean and the lively northern community. "This is where I need to be!" he declared to himself, and it wasn't the kind of idle dreaming we all indulge in while on scenic holidays. He made the Big Change, leaving the desk job and all the trappings of a successful, dull life behind, not an easy thing at all. I have always been averse to feeling trapped myself, so I listened well.

As long as a person was capable of handling radio communications—an operator's course was readily available through the Canadian Sail and Power Squadrons teaching network—and had updated first aid qualifications, they could become a relief lightkeeper. Being handy with tools and machines was a good practical skill to possess, but it wasn't necessary to be a stationary engineer or a heavy-duty mechanic. He mentioned doing weather reports by radio, and that the permanent lightkeepers trained the newcomers, as every station had a different set of visual guides to work with and sometimes different instruments. Doing relief work was a good way to see if the lifestyle appealed on a more permanent basis, he said.

Then I drove off to my appointments and he and his little companion went off to give the lightkeeper at Pulteney Point Lightstation on Malcolm Island his annual holiday break. I now knew that lightkeepers worked seven days a week, for months at a stretch, and that relief keepers were much in demand for medical, dental and family emergencies, as well as for annual holidays.

On the wild and lovely four-hour drive home from Port McNeill to Union Bay the next day, I kept mulling over his practical advice. I remembered how his face lit up when he said how he felt truly, deeply alive upon arriving in Port Hardy.

And wasn't that exactly how I missed feeling? And wasn't that even more the case for my husband, who had dutifully worked at all kinds of low-paying, part-time jobs with awful hours and no benefits or paid holidays for years on end? I at least had an interesting job with great benefits—my first literary job with a dental plan, as I liked to quip. I could read some of the best new books in the English-speaking world in advance of publication, for free, hundreds and thousands of them every year, or go blind trying. But I wasn't doing what I really wanted to be doing with my life and I knew it. My chronic headaches, back spasms and weight gain reminded me constantly that I was out of whack, missing the sizzle and spark and solitude of wilderness and a full-time writing life. I was currently a writer who was too busy selling other people's books to manage more than two Saturdays a month on my own work, hiding myself away behind the Foreign Books section in the Courtenay Library.

Writing is not, as I have patiently explained to a close relative, like darning socks, something you pick up with a happy little sigh of contentment at the end of a long and exhausting day. Writing demands a fresh mind capable of handling what I call creative dichotomy—equal parts intense focus and un-tethered imagination. Some writers flourish at their keyboards by 4:00 a.m., while I ease into full gear by 10:00. Early bird/night owl realities exist and each of us needs to know our peak hours of productivity and to safeguard them if we possibly can... while holding down a job and supporting our families in practical and emotional ways. No small feat, and that's why every book, even if it is not terribly well written or gratefully received or even understood, is a triumph of sheer hard work.

Imagine some poor soul pecking away at a computer like a demented battery hen in a cage, conquering all manner of real and imagined fears, solving problems within their writing—and coping with problems somehow in real life, too—line after line, day after month after year. For many of us, managing to finish a book despite years of multi-tasking and interruptions, with a brain running on sleep-deprived fumes, is the most difficult and the most rewarding task we've ever undertaken. We wouldn't keep doing it if we didn't think of it as the best possible use of our time and talent while we're alive, kicking and relatively compos mentis.

I have to say that despite the modest success of my first two books of fiction in 1990 and 1993, my heart was broken, in several places, during the next busy and frustrating decade and a half of trying to write another book that somebody out there would take a chance on and publish. My very good publishing house was sold and then it went lurching off in other directions that did not include mysteries, so my second book, *Alaska Highway Two-Step*, nominated for an Arthur Ellis Best First Mystery Novel by the Crime Writers of Canada, became a one-off orphan of sorts. My first book, *Disturbing the Peace*, a collection of short fiction, had been one of three finalists for the Ethel Wilson Fiction Prize at the 1991 BC Book Prize Awards. Both books had been on the BC bestseller lists generated by actual bookstore sales as well. It had taken me more than a decade, what with working full- and part-time, to write those two books. Finally, the proverbial last straw: my erstwhile publisher merged with a bigger publisher—one that soon cancelled its Canadian publishing arm entirely.

I was, like many literary orphans in this country, set adrift, and I had lots of illustrious company; there were many good and great writers all looking for new publishers at the same time. Sometimes I've been blessed with wonderful recognition and "luck" in this writing business and sometimes I've been just as haphazardly cursed. I suspect most writers feel this way. It's important to learn how to briskly shake off the negative crap and to carry on writing until our discipline pays off with work so improved, so blazingly good, that it can't be turned down. That's my strategy anyway, and I'm sticking to it.

But I was often too busy to dwell on these dispiriting issues, having met my future partner and collaborator in Life's Great Adventure. What saved me from unknown years of grinding away at writing in isolation was finding a newspaper advertisement for the creative writing department at DTUC (David Thompson University Centre) in Nelson, BC. Jeff George and I were both students at DTUC in what turned out to be its last year of existence. Jeff, a Manitoban writer and photographer with a drought-dry sense of humour, was already in the second year of the diploma program. My one glorious year there exposed me to the nuts and bolts of the Canadian literary market, to great writers like Clark Blaise, Paulette Jiles, Fred Wah and John Newlove, and to visiting greats like Michael Ondaatje, Carol Shields and Alice Munro. Most of all, it informed and restored my decision to choose this precarious, underpaid route to understanding and thinking and living a literary life. Someday I hoped to contribute my own findings. And in the meantime, the first neighbour who welcomed me into her home on Kootenay Lake to talk about writing and theatre was Margaret Stacey, who happens to be, I just recently discovered, a great-granddaughter of Frank and Annie Garrard, the very first lightkeepers on Lennard Island. I am not making this up.

After three years of friendship with Jeff, he and I took a big leap of faith and quickly formed an ad hoc production company to bring Seamus Thomas Woodward-George into the world. Pleased with this excellent collaboration, we carried on working as arts organizers (both), teaching (me) and tree-planting and snow surveying (Jeff). We loved books, art, wilderness and water, old stuff more than new stuff, and we thrived in the lively arts community of the Kootenays.

During a long boat ride from Slocan City one day when Seamus was five years old, we pulled in at the Slocan Lake shoreline near New Denver. It was a sublime blue and green and gold September afternoon as we three walked the quiet streets of the old silver-mining village. Jeff and I noticed more than a few boarded-up or papered-over windows on the main street. We stopped and stared at a vacant two-storey house surrounded by a large lawn with several massive maple trees. It was shabby and in need of TLC but it was obviously solid and had, as builders say, good bones.

We sold our modest 1920 house in Nelson, bought the New Denver house built in 1900, and renovated it to the joists without ever having done anything like it before, thanks to the talents of skilled locals and working many, many long hours ourselves. Seven months later we opened The Motherlode, a book and toy store, which we operated together while raising Seamus for the next eight years.

I kept my shoulder to the family and work wheel, enjoyed singing in the Valhalla Community Choir and organized celebratory book launches for local and touring writers. While on the board of the Slocan Lake Gallery Society, I collaborated with like-minded spirits to create theatre and music projects for teens and professionals and instigated a month-long Migratory Bird Art extravaganza, annual St. Valentine's Poetry Confessionals, Easter Hat Parades and heaven only remembers what else. For two villages of fewer than six hundred people each, Silverton and New Denver have a disproportionate number of generous, community-minded and hugely talented artists in all disciplines.

Jeff was elected to village council twice and served on the board of the Emily Carr School of Art and Design, including a term as chairperson, and I served on the boards and cultural juries of the BC Arts Council, Canada Council, Selkirk College and the Vancouver Foundation. I made a weekly 200-kilometre round trip to Nelson to teach creative writing to adults for the Kootenay School of the Arts and led writing workshops in towns like Nakusp and Revelstoke for Selkirk College and other writing groups.

I managed to write and illustrate a book of short stories for adult literacy students, *Work Is a 4-Letter Word*, in 1999, a contract project for national and provincial literacy organizations, and I wrote occasional articles for newspapers and magazines. I had a little writing office but I was only able to get there two or three times a week, for a few hours at the most, and I was so distracted and just plain tired that I wasn't able to sustain the momentum to produce longer work.

There was also the issue of worrying about our small book and toy store's survival in the lean and mean years of the nineties, when our dollar dipped to sixty-five cents US, the federal government removed the book postage rate (remember being able to mail a book anywhere in Canada for a fifty-eight-cent stamp?) and Chapters and Amazon were flexing their corporate muscles in the low-profit-margin china shop of Canadian independent bookselling.

It was a very difficult time to make a go of it as a small indie bookstore in a village of 526 souls, no matter how many creative events and school book fairs we participated in or organized.

But for Jeff and me, the seven-month building renovation followed by running the bookstore together was an invaluable learning experience, one that strengthened our relationship as partners in all ways. One worked while the other looked after Seamus, and once he was in school, one of us worked on other paid or volunteer work while the other worked in the bookstore. We usually worked shifts: Jeff would open up the store and work until noon and then I'd come in, work the rest of the day and close up shop. We could only afford to hire staff for the busy summer months and December when we were open seven days a week.

By 2001, we knew we had to invent another future for our family, another way of making a better living. Maybe even another adventure would be in store for us. We tried to sell The Motherlode but again, the flukiest sort of luck, both good and bad, befell the few qualified people who made serious inquiries. So we hung on to the building, which has turned out to be a good thing in the long run. Then life offered us an overdue break.

At the very same time as I was emailing one of our publishing friends, Kate Walker, from our apartment to ask if she knew of any available jobs in the book world, she was across the street in our bookstore telling Jeff about a job opening she thought I might be well-suited for! Kate is the (now retired) founder of Kate Walker & Company (renamed Ampersand Inc.), a national company of publishers' sales representatives. One of her reps on Vancouver Island was leaving to own and operate Ivy's Bookshop in Oak Bay so Kate needed another sales rep for Vancouver Island, preferably someone to handle the burgeoning population of the central and north island. Serendipity strikes its silver bell on rare occasions and we knew better than to be deaf to the sound!

I travelled to Vancouver Island to look for a good middle and high school program first. I found the right combination of both in Comox and then busied myself finding a house to rent that was an easy walking distance to both schools. Then I registered Seamus in a week-long catamaran sailing class as a "welcome to the ocean" sort of present. None of us found leaving the Kootenays an easy thing at all and Seamus had already declared that he wouldn't eat seafood, ever. But he was a natural on the water already, an intermediate kayaker by the time he was twelve, a good swimmer and a calm and keen little freshwater sailor.

After six years of coastal living, we'd all made the transition from the Kootenays to Vancouver Island, but it wasn't truly fulfilling for Jeff and me. Seamus was by this time successfully launched. He left home right after his grade twelve graduation to teach sailing to children in Deep Cove, near North Vancouver. He lived in a basement suite, cooking for himself and bicycling to and from the marina. He was seventeen, and we were very proud of him. But after dropping Seamus and a small mountain of groceries at his new place, Jeff and I drove back to the Horseshoe Bay Ferry Terminal, both of us weeping almost all the way there.

How could our boy be grown-up and competent so very suddenly and leave us so soon? We reminded ourselves of friends who had large, ill-tempered twenty- and thirty-something offspring still living in their basements, playing computer games and eating their doting parents out of house and home while not looking for gainful employment. We blew our noses and attempted to be more grown-up ourselves.

Following his summer job, Seamus began an intensive program at Okanagan College in Kelowna to earn his diploma in mechanical engineering. He taught sailing to teens in the Okanagan during the following summer and finished off with an eight-month co-op placement in a boat-building factory. Seamus had raced catamarans in BC throughout his teens—he'd been a *Victoria Times-Colonist* newspaper carrier seven days a week for four years while attending school in Comox and his first big purchase was a used catamaran—and he would later race cats and monohulls all over the world. So we'd done our job as parents, and our drastic move to the Island had allowed us to give him more educational options and skills for his future life.

Maybe it was our turn now, to launch into new adventures, adventures that could give both of us time to write and photograph and paint and grow a garden. I wanted the time again to kayak and maybe do more batik and make quilts. I needed solitary time and I needed wilderness time, and time, most of all, to think and write. Time for new adventures and travel while we were still capable and healthy, if somewhat grey around the muzzles ourselves.

After I finished taking book orders in Alert Bay and Port McNeill, I drove down the Island Highway to the northern outskirts of Campbell River, where there was cell phone reception and was able to leave a message at home: "Get some white wine chilling, honey! I've found out what we're going to do next with our lives. I'm picking up some salmon at the dock in Campbell River!"

During our tasty dinner, I blurted out as many of the details as I could remember about what a would-be lightkeeper needed to do. Jeff's fingers flew over his keyboard until he found the federal government jobs website and the listing for relief lightkeepers. He applied within twenty-four hours, with my unreserved blessings. We'd already been tossing around the idea of someday working as caretakers for fishing lodges and other remote properties where vandals and thieves in boats were an issue. This seemed like a good way to put our toes in the water. I didn't comprehend that I was enabling us to live apart for fourteen long months.

I just wanted Jeff to be happy and to go out on adventurous assignments and to tell me all about them when he got home. Maybe I could even visit him if he worked at a place I could get to by car or ferry, or via station boat if the lightstation was not far off the coast. I wanted him to write stories and to take all kinds of photographs again. Maybe he would learn to play the beautiful old banjo I'd bought him many Christmases ago. Truth be told, I thought maybe I'd write more of my own stories if left to my own devices as well.

I read Don Graham's books about the early history of lighthouses and lightkeepers in this province from cover to cover. I dreamed of finally finishing the novel I'd started in 1995 and about ten other projects on my back burner. Short of committing a serious crime like dropping two tons of long-overdue library books on Stephen Harper's head and then requesting solitary confinement, or shucking family ties and applying to a convent under false pretenses, the lighthouse life was the most appealing one I could imagine for myself as a writer.

During my entire life I've worked all kinds of white-, blue- and even pink-collar jobs to put myself through university and to allow me time and funds to travel and write. I grew up on an isolated Peace River homestead sans electricity, telephone or running water. Many of us who grow up poor, in the material sense, aim for secure, well-paid jobs and vow never to be as chronically cash-starved as our struggling immigrant parents. Meanwhile, reasonably brainy bookworms like myself dream of travelling around the world and discovering how best to be of selfless service to the unsuspecting populace.

Bear in mind I grew up in the sixties and seventies when there were plenty of entry-level jobs in western and northern Canada for bright white girls, although boys who dropped out in grade nine were earning five times as much in the gas and oil fields. Altruistic dreamers with BAS were organizing all sorts of programs to bring young people together with isolated seniors and idealistic youth with inner-city teens as well as starting co-ops of all sorts. On the literary side of things, far, far away from my home in northern BC, young writers and designers were founding little magazines and publishing houses, part of the early seventies surge of creativity in all the arts.

Once I'd leapt off the respectable career tracks I'd tried out during my twenties after graduating from university, I spent years holed up trying to write creatively, rather than in the academic style I had finally adapted to at the University of British Columbia. I worked hard, learned a great deal and even had some fun en route to buying myself writing time and space. I was a farm and home caretaker, a gardener, a waitress, a substitute teacher, an arts organizer, a publicist, singer and sound-effects maker for a horse-drawn theatre company, and a group leader for Canada World Youth in Sri Lanka and India. But it was all a means to get to what I truly wanted to do: write.

Looking ahead, if Jeff liked the lighthouse life and found a permanent position, I knew I'd thrive there. I like physical outdoor work, thanks to growing up on that homestead and plenty of hard labour since then. I am a veteran of road-building and schoolyard excavation work gangs in Sri Lanka, tossing wok-like pans of red tropical dirt and stones down a long line of people for many hours daily, for months. I've laboured long and hard in commercial greenhouses and gardens, and knew I'd love to return to intensive vegetable gardening, as well as thrifty yet creative hobbies like baking bread and making pickles and preserves.

But first and foremost, I'd be able to return to writing.

TWO

Fog Mondo #1

What is so obscure?
Fog, like old fears, dissipates.

Separation Anxiety

ONE DAY IN JUNE 2007, JEFF LEFT OUR SEASIDE COTTAGE IN UNION Bay for an island called Egg, which we'd never even heard of before his posting. After rising at 3:00 a.m., he drove up the North Island Highway and four and a half hours later parked in a long-term Coast Guard spot at the Port Hardy Airport. Shortly after that, he was whisked away by a red and white helicopter. Thus his grand adventure as a relief lightkeeper began, while I carried on working full-time selling to my accounts on Vancouver Island and the Northwest Coast, for by then my sales territory had expanded to Haida Gwaii, Prince Rupert and as far east as Smithers.

Usually, around four o'clock on a home-office workday, I'd expect to hear a knock on my office door.

"Time for a walk," Jeff would say, and I would lift my head up from the computer screen, put on my answering machine and leave my endless to-do list behind. We'd walk down the narrow two-lane highway to the red brick Union Bay post office if I had packages to mail, and then proceed to the old coal port railway trail or to beachcomb along the seashore. We always kept an eye out for black bears intent on devouring apples from the ancient trees near the walking trails.

Without Jeff to distract me, to walk and talk and restore balance to my housebound days, I just kept on working. Jeff has an impish boy inside of him, never too far from the surface of the apparently serious bespectacled and bearded man; a boy who loves to have fun and who takes us, meaning

Seamus and myself, along for the ride. Thanks to the leadership of his Inner Imp, we now are expert planners of extravagantly secretive birthday excursions.

We've ended up on a heritage train in Washington State for a day to celebrate Seamus's ninth birthday, and followed country roads across the Prairies and gotten wonderfully lost, instead of taking the monotonous Trans-Canada. We've gone to an idyllic log cabin in Bamfield and a century-old hotel in Lund. I organized Jeff's surprise fortieth birthday party at Fairmont Hot Springs near the Alberta border, claiming that I was a last-minute replacement workshop leader for a writers' conference there, an elaborate subterfuge that ten-year-old Seamus fully participated in. It was a truly satisfying blind side when the "maids" who barged in the next morning were in fact two of his sisters, one brother-in-law and all of his nieces and nephews, who'd driven from Manitoba to BC to participate.

Jeff and I have a great relationship because we've always been good friends, first and foremost, and we've always been able to talk about anything and everything with each other. We respect each other's brains and hard work because we've slogged through hard physical, mental, emotional and financial times side by side. We are loyal and we have each other's backs unconditionally, which is essential if trust and love are to flourish when hairlines recede (his) and front teeth fall out (mine) and waistlines wax and wane (both). We make each other laugh every day and we both cry during sad movies. We love our son more than anything else on this earth.

So it was a shock for me to suddenly be in an empty house, except for Woodycat, our ancient cat, by turns aloof or affectionate—in short, a normal, nearly non-verbal cat. There were no fun people around to play with. Nobody to yak with in the kitchen as we all hovered around sipping Jeff's good coffee and stirring eggs and making toast for each other. My nest was truly empty.

On some mornings, I'd need to be up even earlier than usual, driving like the proverbial fire-zapped bat to make the first in a full day of appointments in Nanaimo or Tofino or Campbell River. The very thought of going for a walk by myself, after such long days on the road, especially in the face of high winds and pounding rain, did not appeal to me at all. And our location wasn't exactly ideal for popping out for a quick stroll. The sweet oceanfront cottage we rented, smitten by the view from our deck of Baynes Sound and Denman Island, was right beside the narrow, noisy Old Island Highway. No matter that posted signs advised drivers to slow to 60 kilometres through the village of Union Bay, speeders exceeded that advice routinely. Our beloved ten-year-old dog had found his way up there during a second (known) lapse of straying from our fenced yard, following a new furry pal down the beach and up onto the highway one day. It took six sad and expensive weeks for Ben Brown's kidneys to shut down after the hit-and-run driver took off.

I didn't feel completely relaxed walking alone on the woodsy trails, either, without Jeff or our gentle but very large black dog for company. I rode my mountain bike down the old coal port railway bed some days, my heart and feet pumping hard the whole time, or I trudged along the same few village streets a few quiet blocks uphill from the highway. Sometimes I'd swim laps at the ozone-treated aquatic centre in nearby Courtenay, which meant a very early morning or late afternoon for available lap lane times, but the mental and physical relaxation of zoning out (I called it Zenning out) while swimming forty or fifty laps made it all worthwhile.

I actually crave the sensation of really stretching my body out and swimming lap after lap, plowing through the water like a selkie shedding layers of stress. Since I can't exactly swim laps in ocean swells and rough chop, especially with sea lions and orcas lurking in the same ocean, kayaking is now my favourite outdoor activity on salt water. Yet some hardy and intrepid lightkeepers do don wetsuits and snorkels for sorties out into the nippy North Pacific… they are braver souls than I.

Detaching from work-related stress also meant driving to a Comox school for a two-hour choir practice every dark and inevitably rainy Wednesday evening. I'd drive home oxygenated, buoyant, alert and fully alive, thanks to all that singing. It was hard work too, pushing me well beyond my comfort zone. As with the algebra I absolutely loathed in high school, I had to memorize all the theorems and every note of the songs I loved because I couldn't read sheet music. I followed the ups and downs of the notes and knew a full note from a half or quarter note. I knew what a *fortissimo* notation looked like but I couldn't "hear" the notes because I didn't have a keyboard at home to help me. I didn't have childhood music lessons, one of the true regrets of my homesteading European parents, due to living at the end of a winding dirt road made impassable by snow or mud half the year.

One year, from a construction work site, Dad lugged home an abandoned pump organ with most of its white keys out of commission. I taught myself to pick out simple tunes and even a few satisfying chords on the black keys. A community volunteer taught us to play flutophones for several months when I was in grade six. Sometimes in our two- and then three-room school we had teachers with lovely voices, and I remember listening to a fifteen-minute CBC radio program to learn "Frère Jacques" in rounds. Most of the children were too shy to sing the melody, though, let alone learn harmonies. It was much more fun singing to our cows while on board a docile horse, pretending to be an old cowhand from the Rio Grande. Such was the extent of my early music education, except that both my parents could sing well and loved listening to classical music and opera on our battery-operated radio.

For all the choirs I've belonged to for most of my adult life, I used instrumental tapes for the *mezzo*-soprano part to drill the sound of every note and the exact timing of the phrases between my ears. I played the tapes of our concert songs over and over again in my vehicle, singing along, or if I was too tired to manage even that I just listened, to absorb the music by osmosis.

I still have that grade six flutophone out here at the lightstation in 2015. And I miss singing in community choirs very much. Listening to music is fine but it's not the same as making music with others, which is all about being a creator with like-minded people and not just a consumer. Still, Jeff and I both love listening to music, as our CD and vinyl record collections attest, and we now plan most of our holidays to coincide with festivals or much-anticipated live performances. Whenever anyone asks me now what I miss most about life on the Outside, a.k.a. the Rest of the World, I say just two things: singing in choirs and swimming laps.

But then, during those first days and weeks and months of being so far apart from each other, when I looked ahead at our life, I initially thought: five more years. I could do this, I reasoned, lonely though I was. Jeff would be home in a few weeks, then away being a relief lightkeeper for a few weeks at some point again, or a month or two at the most.

And I truly enjoyed my work as a sales rep, busy as I was. Books and book publishing had been central to my existence for two decades. I'd worked as an organizer, publicist and creative writing teacher for the long-running Kootenay Lake Summer School of the Arts, taught adults at the Sechelt Readers and Writers workshop program and worked with talented teenage writers at the Kamloops Young Authors' Conference annually for six years. I taught writing workshops for the Elder Hostel program (which I fully intend to sign up for when I'm older and wiser myself), and I volunteered my organizing and publicity skills for the Kootenay School of Writing in Nelson for nine years as well as teaching creative writing there. I wrote monthly book reviews and artist profiles for several magazines and was a frequent CBC *Daybreak* book reviewer. I also spent five years working part-time in varied editorial capacities at Polestar Press, and I'd been a bookseller for more than ten years between Oliver's Books in Nelson and our own Motherlode Bookstore.

But by this point I had been working as a sales rep for six years, and I just hoped my wobbly lower back and my overloaded brain would continue to cope with the mental and physical demands of my work. Then there was the fact of honouring my own writing, which I could never completely abandon even though the world seemed, like the ocean to a struggling swimmer, remarkably indifferent to my puny hopes and dreams.

I could just keep going to the Bethlehem Centre near Nanaimo for writing retreats for a week or maybe two each year, and then maybe I'd finish yet another rewrite of my contemporary rural BC version of *The Odyssey*. Or finish a new altruism story for a second collection of short fiction concerned with Canadian do-gooders at large, in which I could utilize my experiences as a group home worker, international youth leader and adult protective services worker. It seems to take me at least two decades to process my own experiences thoroughly enough to re-imagine them as fiction. But my confidence in my writing abilities had hit the rocky shoals of despair, and there I floundered.

Every writer, except those who possess buoyant self-confidence due to stunningly good sales, superlative reviews or an enormous ego protected by the hide of a rhinoceros, or those who have high-powered agents begging them for an idea or two scribbled on the back of soon-to-be-legendary envelopes, asks themselves the same hard question: Who gives a crap about these stories I've been slaving over for years except for me? It takes me at least a dozen full drafts of a story to get it right, a process that can take three to five years of effort and fallow time, for which I might find publication in a small Canadian magazine and payment of $150.

And the future of publishing, including my own job in particular, was looking meaner and leaner after the economic and restructuring ravages of the nineties had oozed well into the new millennium. No matter how many Harry Potter books I sold in my rural-marine territory, not to mention all the David Suzuki books and thousands of other brilliant and beautiful and important books, as well as silly, trivial and forgettable books, it was never going to be enough. The big bottom line ruled and 2008 loomed on the financial world's horizon.

I loved my work but I loved writing and Jeff's company much, much more.

THREE

Finding Our Light Choka

radio static
dead air, waiting, to hear you
finish each sentence
faithful, constant, patient you
say "Over" then I flash
shining brightly, steady, true

February

24 Monday
55-311

7:00	1:00
8:00	2:00
9:00	3:00
10:00	4:00
11:00	5:00
12:00	6:00

25 Tuesday
56-310

7:00	1:00
8:00	2:00
9:00	3:00
10:00	4:00
11:00	5:00
12:00	6:00

William

26 Wednesday
57-309   Ash Wednesday

7:00	1:00
8:00	2:00
9:00	3:00
10:00	4:00
11:00	5:00
12:00	6:00

William J Joy

William J Joy

February

20 Thursday
51-315

7:00	1:00
8:00	2:00
9:00	3:00
10:00	4:00
11:00	5:00
12:00	6:00

21 Friday
52-314

7:00	1:00
8:00	2:00
9:00	3:00
10:00	4:00
.00	5:00
12:00	6:00

22 Saturday
53-313

23 Sunday
54-312

●

Fix leaky faucets, toilets, or water pipes.

EcoLogix

Separate Realities

JEFF'S FIRST EMAIL CAME THROUGH FROM EGG ISLAND THE DAY AFTER he arrived there. Hooray for the internet! The modern miracle of technology without which I could not and still cannot function! Jeff was so happy, so utterly thrilled with his new surroundings, and soon he was sending me stunningly good photographs on a daily basis. He was mowing lawns and trimming vast quantities of encroaching salal, and staining and painting and pressure-washing, and getting up at 4:15 a.m. to do the first weather observations of the morning shift. Working as the assistant lightkeeper, he was carrying out these tasks while learning the ropes (a fine old nautical phrase) from the principal keeper, who was a senior keeper stepping in while Egg Island's actual principal keeper was away on an extended summer holiday.

Jeff was living in a large, four-bedroom house with a view of the North Pacific Ocean, out there on the edge of Queen Charlotte Sound. He was seeing humpback whales, orcas, surfing sea lions and all kinds of birds. There was even a peregrine falcon living on the island.

A few days into his posting, he wrote that his relief assignment might last for "a little longer" than the initial six weeks he'd been asked to do. I raced to the nearest mall to put together a care package of his favourite treats: wine gums and chocolate bars, and also work socks and insoles for his gumboots, and some gizmo he'd requested for his computer. Over the long months ahead, there would be many more such care packages, one of which went missing for weeks—and which I, ever the amateur sleuth and customer service specialist, doggedly tracked through a maze of hangars and offices, from Canada Post to the Coast Guard, politely annoying people and alarming my husband, who immediately feared for his future job prospects.

I was genuinely puzzled. How could anyone who spent upwards of nine hours a day brushing back the rainforest jungle and mowing a large, lumpy lawn and sanding and staining hundreds of metres of boardwalk, on top of doing four weather reports seven days a week, fear for his job? The principal keeper, now returned from his vacation, had already put in a good report about Jeff's work ethic and conscientious nature. They watched sports together and occasionally hosted each other for dinners so there didn't seem to be a personality clash or anything like that. But every workplace has its own culture, after all. A little red flag fluttered in a five-knot breeze for me.

Jeff and I would both come to learn, in an extended Life Lesson refresher course, about waiting, and about patience, never our strong suit, while living, working and waiting for certainties on a lightstation. Isolation can magnify the mind's perception of even the most trivial of issues. Think of it as dealing with a problem, say a new hose coupling that doesn't fit the diesel fuel transfer hose. This might score two out of ten in a normal workaday world, a world with weekends to escape to and with other civil and smart people to problem-solve such issues near at hand. In any case, getting the right part might take half an hour, with a cheerful young person behind the wheel of a tiny fuel-efficient car to hand-deliver it to you at your workplace. But on the lights, such a seemingly trivial matter can become a nine out of ten issue.

I was, it seemed, constantly running errands to get parts and items of creature comfort for Jeff's lighthouse life: more camera thingies, computer whatzits, a short-wave radio and socks. Newspapers, magazines, books. More salty and sugary treats. Of course, he'd arrived on Egg with only a duffel bag and enough food for about four weeks. He had set up an account with the Port Hardy Overwaitea before he left in order to have more groceries sent up with the "grocery tender," which was the term for the scheduled helicopter run made once a month to nearly all the Coast Guard lightstations. Some lightstations, like Pulteney Point, Chatham Point and Cape Mudge, were accessible by road—some very rough roads in the case of Pulteney and Chatham, but the keepers there were at least able to drive to nearby towns with grocery stores. The more isolated stations like Egg Island relied on that helicopter run and family or friends to send specialty items not available from the grocery store.

Our ecstatic email communication lasted for eight days until the internet system on Egg Island crashed. This was a major technological challenge. On each and every one of the twenty-seven staffed lightstations on the BC coast, the lightkeepers themselves have installed satellite dishes and set up computer systems. However, problems arise, and the keepers have to figure out their own solutions. The cost of bringing technicians out to the lightstations on water taxis or private company helicopters is prohibitive, and only immediate family members of lightkeepers are allowed to use Coast Guard transportation.

One veteran lightkeeper, now retired, deserves our grateful thanks for every single day we have a functioning web connection because he went off to learn how to set up modems, routers and satellite dishes during his annual leave. Then he taught other lightkeepers how to set up connections on their stations, step by step, from aligning the dish to organizing the rest of the hardware. Thus, he quietly and efficiently revolutionized the isolated lives of Canadian lighthouse keepers. He also helped his First Nations neighbours in their boat- and seaplane-access-only village to join the internet age. Ever since, the COOLTAP (Co-operative Online Temperature and Precipitation Entry System) weather reports have been sent from the lightstations to Environment Canada twice daily via personal computers, and the kelpvine, the keepers' grapevine, has been modernized. Not to mention that Jeff and I were able to be in touch for the sake of keeping our loneliness at bay.

Satellite dishes are needed on most stations for television reception too. Several lightstations are fortunate enough to have landlines, as they are quaintly known in this era of smartphones, but many do not. So lightkeepers have brought in the technology to operate satellite phones and cell phones on those stations that have cell towers somewhere in their mountainous, marine vicinity. It's not nearly as simple as just buying a snazzy cell phone from some porcupine-gelled, big-hair guy in a central mall booth, however.

Jeff and I have now spent many, many hundreds of dollars buying cell phone signal boosters, antennas and hundreds of metres of coaxial cable, plus satellite dishes… so much effort and money for some of the slowest internet and dithering, wavering cell phone reception on the planet. Remember dial-up?

Yup, that's pretty much us. You wouldn't believe what drizzle and fog and near-hurricane-force winds do to reception! But I digress.

When the internet on Egg Island wasn't working, we had to resort to the very public radio phone system to communicate, which every lightkeeper listens to avidly—though some primly deny ever doing so, even whilst their pants are aflame and their noses are elongating. Mercifully, certain ALN (Automated Lighthouse Network) systems, like Egg's, don't allow keepers on the same station to hear each other's transmissions, affording some privacy at least. However, it's much like the rural party lines back in the day for the rest of the circuit of lightstations, except Nosy Parkers don't have to clear their throats, hold their breaths, carefully pick up the receiver and risk neighbourly umbrage when their heavy breathing is detected. Listening in is more entertaining than watching the news about pine beetle infestations or the fate of the Canucks. It's more fun to know that the relief assistant keeper on Egg Island has a nice firm code word for something that his shore-bound wife must miss a whole lot. Oh, undoubtedly.

On the other hand, I can't fathom how intriguing it must be to listen to one adult say "I miss you," followed by a big sigh and crackling silence. "Yeah," the other person admits, aware that ears are pricked for hundreds of kilometres of damp, deserted coastline.

"I miss you too, hon."

No...o...o...o!

You can almost hear the eavesdroppers moan in four-part unison.

"Be specific! What, exactly, are you missing? Describe them/it/hers/his!"

The only good thing about radio phones is that they curbed my awful habit of helpfully finishing Jeff's sentences, and our shared impulsive, impatient, first-born tendencies to interrupt each other. Only one person can speak at a time on this system, and so we lived our parallel lives, with static breaking up our words and dead air dropping them into Queen Charlotte Sound, both of us straining to listen to each other, both of us hanging on.

During the internet hiatus, Jeff also made two short movies on his digital camera, applied a mournful Neil Young soundtrack, put them on disc and got them out to me in the mailbag on a chopper flying south. Even though I wept all the way through them, I laughed as well: the videos showed a furry man with a full-on Viking beard and sun-bleached hair reaching his shoulders. I was looking at an older version of the Jeff who planted trees every summer for five years when we first began our lives together in 1986.

With the radio phone, it was exhausting just trying to carry on a conversation, especially if my brain was poached from being at the computer all day and I had no news to report except: "Overworked, tired, stiff neck and shoulders, oh, and desperately low on blood sugar because I was finally about to stop working and make a Supper for One. Life is not fun."

Jeff was lonely too, despite enjoying his work. He would keep asking me to stay on the line, and to keep talking about something, anything. I told him our son's co-op work placement was going well but he was building motorboats when his abiding passion was sailboats. Woodycat had pulled through what I suspected was ingestion of rat poison from somewhere else. I'd been feeding him warmed milk with an eye dropper and he had rallied. We kept the topics low-key and as neutral as possible using this public form of communication, but after a while, I began to feel that Jeff had escaped dull-normal life and was having all the fun. Forgetting that I'd encouraged him to take the job in the first place, I began to fret that he'd stealthily started a long-term separation process! This is what tired and lonely minds get up to when left to their own devices with no reality check.

He said he was also writing me a long letter on his computer in lieu of daily email, a journal form of letter I would be able to read someday, he hoped. If the internet connection ever got fixed... It didn't, and his initial weeks of relief work carried on and became months. Finally, he asked the Coast Guard office about the possibility of a visit from me, if flights going north and south were convenient, since his relief stint on Egg Island kept being extended and we'd now been apart for two months with no end in sight.

Yes! Permission granted!

FOUR

Finding More Light Choka

Sorrow Bay Grief Point
Sad Rocks Desolation Sound
Old Fears Blind Alley
Morbid Channel Grim Look-Out
Good Hearts Cove Safe Harbour

Egg Island Reunion

NOW I WAS THE ONE UP WELL BEFORE DAWN, DRIVING IN MURKY darkness, my own eyeballs peeled for the glint of deer and elk eyeballs on either side of the North Island Highway en route to Port Hardy. My mind, fuelled by caffeine and adrenalin, raced ahead of my headlights. The joy of taking a complete break from work and being able to fly in a helicopter kept my heart racing. But mainly I wanted to find out if Jeff really loved the life of a lightkeeper and if there was any future for both of us "on the lights," as he referred to his job now. Did he miss me as much as I missed him? He'd better! But the Port Hardy Airport, right beside the ocean, was so fogged in that nothing could take off and all I could do was wait, and hope for an opening in the skies. And attempt to catch some sleep on the musty old couch in the Coast Guard hangar waiting room.

My bags and a cooler were packed with warm work clothes, smoked salmon and frozen spot prawns from Royston, where I bought them directly from a fishing family. Greek olives nestled beside wine gums, walnuts and a bottle of hot sauce. I included the most recent issues of BC *Book World, The Walrus, Harper's, Esquire, Geist, The Atlantic Monthly, The New Yorker* and *Quill & Quire*. All our literary staples. Jeff had been writing reviews of mysteries for *Q&Q*, a Canadian publishing trade magazine, for the past several years. Somewhat sadly, his isolated work location made the logistics of getting him advance review copies in time to meet deadlines next to impossible, so that ended an interesting freelance gig.

I crammed in *The Book of Clouds*, the *Audubon Field Guide to Weather* and a few advance reading copies of new novels. I was also in the midst of reading a brilliant book by Vancouver writer Bruce Grierson called *U-Turn: What If You Woke Up One Morning and Realized You Were Living the Wrong Life?* Serendipity in book form, you might say. He documented the stories of over three hundred people who made profound 180-degree shifts in their lives, which reminded me of the high-ranking civil servant with the Jack Russell terrier I'd met en route to his relief lightkeeper posting. It is a book rich with examples of people, ranging from Mahatma Gandhi to relatively unknown and magnificent citizens, who waged peaceful, determined battles to improve the lot of other living beings and the planet itself, people who listened to their inner voice or someone else's ringing truths and responded by changing their own lives to suit their new purpose in Life. Grierson also touches on why and how people on this earth are connected within six degrees of each other. I swear Canadians are connected by 1.5 degrees at most. I'd written an article about discovering Nelson, BC, for Bruce when he was the editor of *Western Living* magazine only a few years earlier, but have yet to meet him in person to say how important his book was to me.

What else did I pack? Newspapers, the ones that still had book review sections, like the Saturday *Vancouver Sun* and *Globe and Mail*, as well as the vacuum cleaner bags needed by the principal keeper, and the electric hair clippers Jeff used to cut his own hair.

The fog started to lift by noon and by 1:00 p.m. I could hear the wonderful thumping drone of an approaching helicopter. My heart thumped back in response. At last! I climbed aboard for my second helicopter ride ever and up and away we went, flying over the dense coastal forests, some with mountains logged off like the tonsures of medieval monks. Then we went "heli-surfing", flying low over frothy ocean swells and gleaming, deserted beaches, with only an occasional fishboat or tugboat far offshore. The friendly pilot chatted away, pointing out old logging camps and an elegant navy blue Alaska-bound ferry. Thirty-five minutes later we hovered over the cement helipad extending from the forested oval of Egg Island.

I had a hard time restraining tears when I saw Jeff waiting near the helipad. He'd lost weight and the part of his face I could still see above his sandy-red Viking beard was deeply tanned. We were a bit shy about being

Jeff's first sighting of Egg Island Lightstation in Queen Charlotte Sound.

publicly affectionate so we hugged quickly, hard, while the principal keeper discreetly whisked away my luggage in a wagon attached to a small tractor.

We had ten whole days to finally pour out our unedited thoughts and feelings! To explore the island from top to bottom, to explore each other likewise, to make lovely meals for two, to hang out and talk for hours. We were just so happy to be together again. All our doubts about this prolonged separation faded into the background. There was time, too, to visit back and forth with Harry, the principal keeper, another prairie lad and very hospitable baker of muffins and cakes. I tromped along with Jeff every three hours on his afternoon shift weather reports to learn how to read the skies and the seas, to decipher the thermometers inside the Stevenson screen, to study the Beaufort wind scale and to listen silently as the most northerly lightstations called in their reports to the Prince Rupert-based weather station.

Egg Island was in the middle of two Coast Guard radio zones. "Good evening, Lights," the weather collector's voice from MCTS (Marine Communications and Traffic Services) in Prince Rupert began, and I listened to the Langara, Green, Bonilla, Triple, McInnes, Boat Bluff, Ivory, Addenbroke and Dryad lightstation weather reports. Then Comox MCTS collected the reports from the lightstations at Pulteney Point, Scarlett Point, Egg Island, Pine Island, Cape Scott and Quatsino.

"Thank you. Good night, Lights," the cheerful radio voice signed off when the last weather reports were taken at 10:30 p.m.

"Good night, Lights!"

Imagine hearing that next time you are on a fishboat, tugboat, sailboat, yacht, cruise ship or ferry going up the BC coast to Alaska and you see the sweeping bands of light from a lighthouse in the dark, all by itself. Wish us all a good night. Whenever I look out now and see a lone boat on the horizon, I sing "Good night, brave little boat" into the dark void. Even when I know the boat is a massively powerful beast of a tugboat, we all know the ocean is the biggest beast of all.

My imagination was transported by all the voices on the radio: gruff, hesitant, upbeat, subdued, officious, terse. All the staffed lightstations were becoming real to me, more than just labelled sites on the map I had seen online on the Lighthouses of British Columbia site. The complex geography of the coastline meant that each station often had very different weather conditions to report, for example. Whoever put the lighthouses where they were had obviously relied on mariners' advice about hazardous zones. I studied the nautical charts on the walls in Egg Island's radio room while Jeff did his dew point calculations and prepared his written notes for the radio reports. There were islands as numerous as freckles on a redhead in these North Pacific waters, beginning with the Broughton Archipelago to the south and extending to the Aleutian Islands off Alaska.

Sorrow Island. Grief Bay. Both places were on nearby Calvert Island. I could only imagine what led to those names. I've always loved maps and charts and now my imagination, fuelled by restorative eight- to eleven-hour sleeps, was happily swooping and spiking and synthesizing. It had been a long, long time since I'd felt this happy, beloved, rested, alive and just plain content.

There were three houses as well as outbuildings on Egg Island and the weather was, happily, dry and almost warm, though the winds off the ocean were always cool. While Jeff worked during the day shift, I admired the white Shasta daisies and the blue Siberian irises that flanked the cement walkways, the two small greenhouses, the pristine white, red and grey Coast Guard buildings and the recently stained (by Jeff's fair hand) boardwalk to the far end of the island where sea samples were collected daily at high tide. Beside the boardwalk stood a tall tree with an immaculately painted and varnished sign, The Haven 4 Lost Soles, festooned with decrepit running shoes, frayed workboots and de-Velcroed sandals. These were not, as I'd originally thought, spewed up by the ocean onto the island's few rocky beaches, but were recent donations of used and abused footwear from the current generation of light-keepers on Egg Island.

When I was in Union Bay, I slept fitfully, with a baseball bat within reach—there were frequent vehicle thefts and break-ins, even one at my neighbour's house a mere three metres from my own front door, due to the easy opportunities afforded by the nearby highway. I'd yelled at a brazen fellow on a bicycle who'd pulled into our empty carport (my vehicle was in the Union Bay garage getting work done). He stopped poking through my recycling bin and pedalled away fast. Those days, I missed the company of our devoted, deep-voiced dog more than ever.

I slept and slept on Egg Island, with only the sounds of the wind in the evergreens, the cries of the sea birds and the comforting push and pull of the ocean swells. One night humpback whales circled the island, singing their eerie whale songs, some *basso profundo*, others swooping up into the heldentenor range. I had to pinch myself.

Imagine falling asleep to whales singing deep sea lullabies.

I had to find a way to live this life. I was constantly putting my binoculars up to my eyes, held captive by the natural displays around me. One day I was unable to tear myself away from watching the athletic, long-flippered humpback whales breaching and bubble-netting in a group of seven or eight, with a frantic swirling mass of small fish trapped inside their circle. This is sometimes called echelon feeding because the whales work as a team, several of them underwater releasing air bubbles, which the panicked fish swim away from, only to encounter the giant maws of the waiting whales at the surface of the water, or the next level, hence, echelon.

Imagine whales controlling their underwater burping so cleverly as to produce a steady column of bubbles to control fish! (Warning: Do not attempt this manoeuvre with your fishing buddies no matter how much beer has gone down your hatches.) While we watched this phenomenal sight, a northbound float plane circled overhead, watching the same spectacle from its superb vantage point. And by great good chance, the *Gordon Reid*, one of the Coast Guard's ships, was also in the 'hood and sent out a Zodiac to bring their scientists and cameras even closer.

We envied them from our distant spot on the Egg Island helipad, armed with our binoculars and a telescopic camera lens not quite up to the task. We could only imagine what the sight of whale heads and open mouths the size of Honda Civics would look like from a few metres away.

Another day I watched a pod of flashy, speedy orcas leaping out of the water, breaching to show us their black and white tummies, performing for the sheer glee of it, as far as I could tell. I've since learned that whales like humpbacks and orcas may breach for display reasons ("Check out this gleaming torso, ladieees…"), to show displeasure ("See this massive flipper? Don't make me slap you upside the head…"), to shed skin parasites ("Yuck! Get *off* this pristine bod!"), or even to inhale water-free air in rough seas by getting as far up and out of the water as possible before gulping air into their lungs. That last reason makes a lot of sense to me. They could have been practising their acrobatics for exactly such life-saving air supply manoeuvres. Smart, smart mammals.

While we know that whales talk and sing to each other, we, meaning scientists, have yet to learn all the vocabulary and nuances of their language. We do know, however, that the barrage of underwater explosions during weapons testing by the military ships of the world and the thumping of ship engines is an incredible assault on the sensitive hearing of whales and other marine mammals. Soon, I hope, we'll understand their pleas, if we're smart enough, and if there are enough scientists left at Environment Canada who are still funded to study whales and allowed to speak publicly about this issue and other inconvenient truths. As a taxpayer, I'd like to know all about their scientific findings without any censorship by politicians whose financial backers do not want voters to know about the true costs and environmental damage potential of their mega-projects.

Canada's federal government downgraded the protected status of humpback whales as an endangered species in 2014. The timing is fishy, of course. In 1966, when this whale was first protected from slaughter by the international whaling fleet, then primarily Japanese and Norwegian whalers, fewer than a thousand humpbacks were known to live in the entire North Pacific, migrating between Hawaii, Mexico, Baja California, British Columbia and Alaska. In 2014, it was estimated that six thousand humpbacks lived in this area. However, the currently Conservative Canadian federal government is determined to ram through assorted pipeline projects that will take tar sands bitumen from Alberta to Asian ships at Pacific ports. Those ships will then use the habitat of British Columbian salmon and several species of migratory whales as shipping lanes. It is not a done deal, however. Far from it.

But I digress.

Back on my own personal Happy Mini-Planet of Egg Island, I watched the oystercatchers pry into mussels with their amazing pointy beaks and I began the task of identifying one gull from another, inseparable even with the help of my bird book and binoculars. Or I'd sit on the helipad and laugh at the sweet smiles on the faces of surfing Steller sea lions, mostly young males. These Steller surfer dudes would play for hours on end in the heavy westerly swells. Once I counted nine dudes in the line-up!

Steller sea lions, Steller's jays, Steller's eider ducks... they led me to the world of physician, botanist, zoologist and explorer Georg Steller. Steller was the first known non-Native to set foot on Kayak Island, one of many North Pacific islands that are now part of Alaska, on July 20, 1741. Because he'd seen drawings and descriptions of the American blue jay, he was able to identify its cousin in the north and to make an educated guess that the ship he was on, captained by Vitus Bering of sea and strait fame, was very near the continent of North America. He persuaded Captain Bering to grant an extended ten-hour layover on Kayak Island, where they stopped to take on fresh water, in order to conduct observations of land and sea fauna and take samples of the island flora.

Steller, a German by birth, was eventually recalled to the Russian capital of St. Petersburg because he was "too sympathetic" to Native islanders being brutalized by the Russian crew, even though he'd saved a number of the men from scurvy with his vitamin C teas derived from dried berries. Those who scoffed at his remedies and refused to take them died. Do remember to tell this true story if your own kids don't want to swallow their vitamins.

Two of the species Steller identified, the Steller sea cow and the spectacled cormorant, soon became extinct due to European over-hunting of the placid creatures. But his name lives on, and to me he seemed like a remarkably prescient and progressive person.

More notes to self: Study oceanography. Buy *Plants of Coastal British Columbia*. Buy more northern maps and charts. Reread the chapter on Egg Island in Donald Graham's *Lights of the Inside Passage*, an astonishing litany of deaths by misadventure (usually drowning), near-deaths by starvation and near misses, as when entire buildings, including the 1898 Egg Island lighthouse, were swept off their foundations by rogue waves.

Stern note to self after rereading the last chapter: stop whining about the lack of internet service, for heaven's sakes! Consider watching helplessly as the supply ship heaves up and down offshore in a relentless storm (with twelve dozen eggs smashed and the salt pork and hams turning a fetid greyish-green). The captain unwilling to risk the lives of his crew to row a smaller boat in to deliver the mail and somewhat edible food, which only happened two or three times a year... So the keepers and their hungry families had to watch and wait and pray for calmer seas. There is no safe harbour on Egg Island, surrounded as it is by reefs. The lightstation exists to warn all boaters to keep well away from the place.

Speaking of light, the contemporary "lighthouse" on Egg looks like a Meccano set project perched on the island's highest hill, all metal struts, four columns and a built-in ladder, with a banal sort of revolving apparatus on top housing a minimalist light bulb. But it gets the job done and only a tsunami of the most astounding height would ever reach it, unlike two of its more picturesque predecessors knocked off their foundations.

And a P.S. to self: don't kvetch about cramped living quarters anywhere, ever again. Remind yourself of the Wilkins family in November 1948 after a tsunami demolished the Egg Island lighthouse (again), which was built in the early style. The cupola and light were built on top of the keeper's house. After the shock of the tsunami, the family members were clad only in pyjamas for five days, huddled in the chicken coop. Mr. Wilkins hung a kerosene lantern in a tree and a passing boat noted a small light "at low level" and then saw the waterborne carnage of the main building. When the violent storm subsided the family was finally rescued, suffering from hypothermia and hunger. And a P.P.S. to self: always have an escape plan, or several such plans, with first aid kits and food and water caches in the mix. In fact, every dwelling on the BC lightstations has a complete earthquake kit packed and ready to go near one of the exits, rope ladders if needed, and an early warning and evacuation plan in place for tsunamis and other natural disasters.

But this was August 2007 and the sun shone on a benign ocean surrounding the green oval of Egg Island. I watched as awkward pigeon guillemots attempted water landings, lurching and floundering every time—such unbalanced little birds, but could they ever swim underwater, in their true element. The resident peregrine falcon was a whirring sound and then a brown blur. I never did get a good look at it. I'd never heard or seen so many giddy, raucous oystercatchers either, with their red legs, orange beaks and yellow-lined eyes contrasting with their shiny black feathers. They laid their eggs haphazardly in the rocks, counting on the chicks' mottled grey and black camouflage to save the day while they winged off on late afternoon fly-pasts, the entire flock shrieking their heads off the whole time. They shrieked only a little more when they came back to discover that seagulls and crows had scooped up their new hatchlings. I wanted to report them to the authorities for extreme laissez-faire parenting but obviously some chicks survived long enough to continue propagating the species.

One day, while out walking and birdwatching, I saw a line of dense whitecaps far out on the ocean, coming from the northwest, and watched as it came closer. I assumed it was wave action, pushed by strong offshore winds, as I was used to watching out for the infamous "black line" on Slocan Lake in the West Kootenays. The black line there was a wall of fresh water being pushed by strong northern winds, a water wall that grew rougher and higher the farther it was pushed down the narrow but deep mountain trench. One look at that ominous black line and canoeists, kayakers, sailors and anyone messing about in smaller motorized boats scooted for safety in a hurry.

But as I kept watching this broad expanse of frothing whitecaps, I saw something twirling in the midst of the front row. Then more things leaping straight into the air and twirling, upright dancing on water, leaving rooster-tail wakes! Soon I was able to recognize Pacific white-sided dolphins—a super-pod of several thousand, we estimated. This awesome sight, as well as the cooperative bubble-netting manoeuvres of the humpback whales, made me feel like I'd stepped into my own personal *Nature of Things* documentary.

Behind the house Jeff lived in was a trail we followed to a small clearing protected by spruce trees. Jeff showed me the white picket fence surrounding the grave of Laurie Dupuis, a keeper who committed suicide on Egg Island in the 1950s. It was a sad story of misreading the punctuation in a terse telegram (a sharp-eyed, nitpicking copy editor at the telegram office might have saved a man's life by swapping a comma and a period), of Mr. Dupuis struggling with jealousy after a long, hard winter on the island with just his common-law wife and stepson for company, a winter filled with bickering by all accounts. His wife and her son had left the island for a month in order for her to undergo minor surgery in a city hospital. One day, while he was still all alone on Egg Island, Mr. Dupuis received a telegram.

Here is the telegram as read by the radio operator at Bull Harbour, containing no salutation or proper name of the intended receiver: "I MUST HAVE PICTURE OF YOU. RECEIVED YOUR LETTER. JUNIOUR, GOOD LUCK."

How was Mr. Dupuis to know that the letter was addressed to his stepson, not his wife? Who was "Juniour" [sic]? Did Laurie Dupuis, whose second language was English, assume someone called Juniour was smitten with his temporarily absent wife, or that she was writing and reuniting with her former husband, when in fact the letter was written by the latter to their son—whom he would naturally call Junior? Dupuis's death by his own hand was the very saddest of interpretations and responses. This tragedy finally spurred the federal government department of the day in charge of lighthouses to ensure that every station have at least two keepers on duty, with relief keepers brought in without fail to fill in for any full-time keeper called away for medical or family emergency reasons.

Every Egg Island lightkeeper since has tended his grave and, no doubt, pondered abandonment, miscommunication and despair. Jeff and I had endured our small rough patch of that, in fact, and without email to communicate privately and only the frustrating technology of public radio phone outreach, old wounds had festered and erupted. Thankfully, we had more than twenty years of loyal friendship to steady us through the jagged reefs of our own creation. We truly disliked living apart from each other for more than a few weeks. We did not ever want to "get used to it." But for the time being, we made the most of the precious days we had together, and I started writing about birds, using Japanese poetic forms.

I marvelled at the Egg Island greens Jeff had transplanted, having rescued them from greenhouse starter pots before they keeled over. He tended them carefully and fourteen prime heads of lettuce, as pretty as oversized green roses, were the proud result. I found myself making futuristic garden plans with one of the island greenhouses as the key to my success. The island's short, cool growing season was compensated for by the longer daylight hours at that northern latitude. I was once a 4-H Happy Harvester, after all, and I've been a lifelong gardener, always yearning for a greenhouse and a decent patch of land. A greenhouse, a writing room of my very own, a climbing rose and an asparagus patch... was it too much to hope for, sooner rather than later in this life?

I also loved the old-fashioned, spacious Coast Guard house with its vast kitchen countertops and full-length covered verandah. I fancied warm Swedish colours and made sketches, adding notes about buttery yellows and pale blues and sage greens. A bit of cherry red on some crisp, striped kitchen curtains, perhaps. Farmhouse, yet with a nautical touch. Well, I was off to the races, wasn't I, busily decorating with a sumptuous Gibbs-Smith book on seaside cottages as a reference.

Jeff sat me down at his computer on Day Three of my ten-day visit. I read his journal, a long letter to me, several hundred pages' worth amassed over six weeks. I laughed. I cried. I looked at his amazing photographs, hundreds of them. I was so happy for him, to know that he was back in touch with his creative self and that he was in such a stimulating environment. This light-keeping work was exactly right for him. There was only one overall element missing. Me.

FIVE

Oystercatcher Somonka

I approach sideways
Yellow-ringed eyes, shy, downcast
My head bows to you.

Mmm, that neon beak!
What a man! Let's fly, let's shriek
Giddy mate of mine!

Social Butterfly
Contemplates Migration

THE BIGGEST HELICOPTER IN THE COAST GUARD FLEET, A SOUTH-bound Sikorsky capable of carrying over thirty people, touched down on the Egg Island helipad, barely fitting onto it. My depleted packsack and I boarded, and all too soon we roared up and away, leaving behind the waving lightkeepers and the perfect oval island surrounded by the wild North Pacific Ocean. My heart was heavy but I was relaxed and my mind was clear. The future I imagined was possible. I just had to be patient.

I still loved at least 80% of my publishing job. I was actually being paid to do what the French call cultural animation, and I loved helping get my authors to festivals and bookstore and library events, pitching in to help my booksellers sell books, finding weird props and costumes, and just making fun stuff happen in my literary world. Even in high school, I thrived best doing behind-the-scenes organizing to create a three-day Roaring Twenties Festival. Or invading a Rotary Club meeting with the geography class (thanks to the collusion and encouragement of our deceptively straitlaced teacher) in Fort St. John to sing a catchy protest song, most of which I'd written, about how wrong it was to dump raw sewage into the Peace River. *"P" is for the Peace we love so dear... "E" is for Effluent dumped much too near...*

So I'm a choir sort of person, not a soloist, unless forced into it. Really, it's less nerve-wracking and much more fun to be dancing the Charleston with nine other friends on the back of a flat-deck truck for an hour-long parade through Fort St. John than it ever would be to attempt a solo tap dance for the talent show. I don't have the right shoes. Or an overwhelming need for constant attention, either. The limelight might glance off me every once in a while but I don't waste my precious time lunging after its fickle beam of approval. Collective wisdom is really the only kind we have: six heads are better than one and besides, it's all about having more fun with more people involved.

The book business is chock a block with smart, imaginative, funny, hard-working people in every single area, from authors to illustrators, designers, editors, marketing and publicity wizards, book reps, front line booksellers, even the CEOs and the publishers paying the bills. We are, all of us, Children of the Book. As they say in the theatre, "There are no small roles, only small people." Only the terminally small-minded fail to get the gist of this wisdom.

Selling books is a massive team effort from start to finish and if I was going to choose the isolated life of a lightkeeper's wife and occasional relief keeper, I would be leaving interesting work with all these bright live wires. I'd also be leaving decent pay, regular holidays and extended health benefits, all of which I'd rarely had in my adult life. But I guess that's what I get for choosing writing as my lifelong passion and working at seasonal, short contract and part-time jobs to buy myself writing time, instead of strapping on the harness, complete with blinders and muzzle, and embarking on a sensible, well-paid career with a fat pension.

For starters, now that we had established that Jeff liked the lighthouse life and the working conditions, he needed a permanent position before I could quit my job. Seamus had almost finished his first stretch of post-secondary studies but I wanted to be available to help him in the critical transition to either his first full-time job or moving on to undertake a degree. We didn't want to choose a totally isolated lightstation, either, where it would be difficult for him to visit or for us to get out to see him, or even to communicate. And in 2007 both Jeff and I had mothers who were in their late seventies and we wanted to be able to visit them with a reasonable amount of ease, especially if a medical emergency occurred.

But there were rumours circulating on the kelpvine about positions opening up, and if the news was valid, Jeff's timing was, at last, hallelujah, cue Etta James, fantastic. We just had to wait and see. I decided to go to night classes and crammed in some weekend sessions to get my radio operator's certificate and my standard and marine first aid certification. I also updated my tetanus shot. As I said, I've always liked having a Plan B. And a Plan C in reserve, like a current passport.

Even in those early days, before we'd both worked on over a dozen different lightstations between us, we knew that every station has its pros and cons. In 2007, we could look at photographs of the various lightstations on websites, but of course these were often limited to prosaic shots of the actual light tower and overhead shots of the station and its red, white and grey buildings. Picturesque, and nearly always shot in the fleeting and glorious sunshine of summer, but not all that useful in ascertaining whether a place was suitable for us. As a new relief keeper Jeff had limited access to the kelpvine, and only a few hasty opinions from other keepers he chatted with in transit. It seemed as though we were plotting our future course based on how difficult it would be for me to get out to the lightstation in question, most of all. We knew helicopter visits would likely only be possible very few times a year and even then, would be weather dependent. We had to find a location that didn't present a major transportation obstacle, first and foremost, if we were to continue living separately.

Here's what we compared in a hypothetical either/or fashion when we knew next to nothing about the lighthouse life:

- proximity to medical expertise, or true marine wilderness and isolation
- great halibut and salmon fishing, or prawn or Dungeness crab nearby (either choice meant a real dock and the chance to have our own boat again)
- excellent, well-tended garden beds and greenhouses, or rocky, acidic, neglected soil requiring intensive labour and applications of seaweed and compost to correct the pH balance in order to grow a bean, or even a pea
- a spacious house with a 360-degree ocean view but with the wind chill permeating its seams, or a snug, sheltered house with limited ocean views
- frequent helicopter or lifeboat mail and freight deliveries, or one or two helicopters a month at most

- great kayaking or rowing opportunities, versus taking your life into your hands if you ventured out on any form of flotation 90% of the year
- the sound of sirens and the sight of city lights in a dry-ish microclimate, or the open North Pacific, true wilderness and relentless rain a good nine or ten months of the year
- wonderful, long hiking trails, or a ten- or twenty-minute stroll around a tiny barren or heavily wooded island
- blissful silence and hours to write and to garden every summer, versus hundreds of hikers and other visitors every week, all asking the same three questions
- the tang of iodine, cedar and salt in the air, or loads of sulphuric sea lion urine floating in every time a southeaster blows, or a cormorant rookery a stone's throw from the porch with fishy guano odours so strong one's eyes instantly emit tears in self-defence

I also knew I needed to be able to get out, by some reliable means, in order to work as a writer again, to give public readings and do school tours, to perform at festivals and to sign books in bookstores and all the things I used to do in the early nineties when my first two books were published. Now, kick-starting my writing life all over again, I would also need a website. Or a blog, apparently. Also, Facebook, LinkedIn and Twitter. Not that those prospects appealed to me. Who had time to write or even *think* when they were so busy blathering on for free about me-me-me, sell-sell-sell to the universe? Who had time to read everyone else's blogs and tweet other twittering twits? Not me. I had fifteen years of catching up on writing to do. Clearly, I would have to be hauled, kicking and yowling, into the twenty-first century. I was the last kid in grade six to adopt a ballpoint pen for school use, using my traditional "stick" ink pen, blotter and ink bottle, all writing paraphernalia I loved, for one rebellious, overdue day.

In any case, I knew I needed a reliable internet connection in order to pitch my work to magazines and publishers, or to work as a book reviewer, or to go back and forth with editors on my own manuscripts. Oolichan Books had expressed interest in seeing more of my *Odyssey* novel, and Simply Read Books was planning on bringing out my first children's picture book, *Singing Away the Dark*. (Certainly doing things like coordinating a multi-event tour for both books in sixteen BC towns, cities and villages in the fall of 2010 could only have happened because I had email.)

Early lightkeepers are snorting, cussing and/or twirling like Pacific white-sided dolphins in their graves at this statement, no doubt, given their extra-Grimm reality of waiting for mail, food and newspapers every three to six months. But that was then—in the era of the telegram, at best. In this era, we happily photograph our cheques on our smartphones and instantly deposit them in our credit union account instead of waiting weeks for the next lifeboat to brave the swells and storms.

Jeff and I had a lot to consider, and did as much research as we could into the prospective postings. What we've since learned, of course, is that getting along with the one or two other inhabitants of a lightstation is the single most critical factor of all, far more important than the microclimate or access to the nearest airport. A harmonious living and working relationship is a total crapshoot, to quote an O.W.L. (Old Wise Lightkeeper). It's best to keep a respectful personal space and "just work it out, as far as workload goes." This falls into the easier said than done category of wisdom, of course, depending so much on the life experience, work ethic and tendency toward autocratic tyranny or utter sloth in the two individuals trapped on the same green rock.

Add to the possible mix that a rookie assistant lightkeeper might find him- or herself tiptoeing into, all stuck on one island for weeks and months on end, with years stretching before them: a wild variety of religious and spiritual persuasions; people who want all the available garden land for themselves; people who hoard information, expertise and equipment (knowledge is control, or at least the illusion of world domination); extroverts trapped in the wrong occupation; people with no people skills who have never supervised other people becoming supervisors; those who suddenly reveal their Insecure Tyrant Persona when given an intoxicating piece of turf to reign over; and yes, thankfully, well-balanced, emotionally secure, intelligent people who gladly share information and expertise, who observe and respect shift work and time off-duty, who are a joy to be around and who also happen to do a very conscientious job as lightkeepers.

But we knew little of these crucial realities at the start and so we endlessly reviewed our criteria and waited. Jeff's relief work on Egg Island stretched out to four and a half months. I was able to visit by helicopter for another eight days at Thanksgiving, where I made a feast for all three inhabitants, complete with classic orange candles, a proper tablecloth and a great bottle of Wild Goose Gewurztraminer I'd won for writing a short travel piece. By this time the internet service on the station was repaired and Jeff and I were not nearly so desperately lonely for each other's good company, thanks to our daily emails.

Both of us stood on the same sad Shores of Resignation, though, accepting the necessity of living apart but not liking the long view at all. Some lightkeepers and their partners spend years living like this, only seeing each other for a few weeks or a month or two at most every year. Neither of us ever wanted to get used to that lukewarm love life. The weeks and months dragged by and we soldiered on in our respective jobs.

But just as the West Coast Winter monsoons set in with a vengeance, other skies opened to pour some sunshine on our behalf. Our timing, for once, was bang on. The kelpvine was accurate! A goodly number of lightkeepers who had started out in the seventies and eighties, and who'd survived several rounds of lighthouse automation and de-staffing in the eighties and nineties, were now retiring. A competition for an unprecedented number of assistant keeper postings, five all at once, was finally announced.

Jeff wrote the exam, was interviewed and then qualified. Some keepers did relief work for years before permanent positions ever opened up so we were pleased, to say the least, for the opportunity after only four and a half months. He is the most genuinely modest person I have ever known but I can state without undue bias that he is both intelligent and hard-working.

Jeff had three choices offered to him and he chose Trial Island, near Victoria, for its proximity to me, just two and a half hours' drive away, and to Seamus, who had nearly wrapped up his co-op program to graduate with his engineering diploma. Seamus was eager to find boat-related work on

Vancouver Island and to resume his own passion, racing sailboats. Where better than Victoria or nearby Sidney to fix boats and race them?

Certainly the access to Trial Island, by station boat to and from the Oak Bay Marina, near Victoria, would make our lives much easier.

SIX

Cormorant Choka

Out on jagged reefs
perch undertakers, dark birds
wings half-open, still
drying them, or trying to.
Patient, perhaps kind
not like some, all braying cheer
and false bonhomie
shoving through our swells of grief
to bury strangers.

Allow this world its sorrows
like cormorants, leave us be.

Life on Trial

So JEFF LEFT REMOTE AND WILD EGG ISLAND, WITH SOME PANGS AND misgivings, and moved to Trial Island Lightstation in November of 2007 with only the most essential sticks of furniture, kitchen utensils and books. Our fifteen-year-old bookstore cat was also sent over from our Union Bay cottage to keep Jeff company. From within his travel crate, Woodycat objected most vociferously to the helicopter noise.

There were some concerns about an old cat on a barren island without a lot of hiding spots, with plenty of eagles cruising around and an evil-looking pack of river otters. And everyone except us fretted about the other keeper's dogs. Woodycat was a street cat we'd rescued in Nelson who proceeded to hang lickings on any dog of any size that went after him, and to evade all other predators coming by land, sea or sky.

Two weeks after Jeff was transferred, I was able to get over to Trial Island from the Oak Bay Marina on a sturdy fibreglass boat driven by the principal keeper. It was a twenty-minute ride over a light chop of less than a foot with no discernible swell on a rare calm and sunny day in late November. I remarked that Jeff would really enjoy handling a boat again as he'd grown up with them and we'd enjoyed our years on Kootenay and Slocan Lakes with an old Park Ranger Aroliner aluminum powerboat and a fibreglass sailboat of unknown vintage.

Once the station boat was winched to safety in the boathouse, a beaming Jeff waiting on terra firma helped pack my stuff (more lovely Royston prawns, chocolate, newspapers, naughty nightwear instead of my usual sturdy flannel

PJs, and for the eternal boy, wine gums too) over to his new digs. He showed me around the assistant keeper's house, another variation of the three basic Coast Guard housing types. This one was a small two-bedroom house with a full basement, and previous keepers had done a wonderful job of remodelling the kitchen and the bathroom. It was a sweet little house with a lived-in and well-loved feeling, even though Jeff's furniture was minimal—or as he called it, packing box decor.

From the house there was an excellent view of the Olympic Mountains range in Washington state from two windows, but to get the full picture of how high the seas were running in the Juan de Fuca Strait, it was necessary to walk up to the principal keeper's house on the highest point of elevation, only a five-minute walk away. The radio room was the size of a large cupboard or, more accurately, a small porch, attached to the side of the house. There the anemometer was kept, as well as the weather logbook, the lightkeepers' log, some files and manuals and the radio phone for the daily weather reports.

This lightstation was one of very few stations connected to the electricity grid of Vancouver Island so there was no "tank farm" of diesel fuel tanks. There was an engine room with one engine in it and a small fuel tank as backup in case the electrical connection to Vancouver Island failed. Occasionally some barrels of fuel were slung from the deck of a Coast Guard ship to Trial Island by helicopter, but unlike an all-diesel station, there were no labour-intensive refuelling operations with Coast Guard ships and their fuel barges carrying tanks of diesel, or heavy hoses to haul up rough terrain to the on-site fuel line. At some stations like Estevan Point, where the sturdy barge cannot get close enough to do the job, a helicopter has to sling bladders of fuel from ship to shore, which always makes for very long days.

The toilets here were saltwater flush, not composting, and since as early as 1910 the station had had its own phone line via submarine cable, so as far as mod cons went, Trial Island was truly state of the art. One writer friend has noted how often I include the particulars of toilets in nearly all my published

Woodycat the lighthouse cat joined the family as a kitten in Winlaw, BC and lived almost nineteen years. This photo was taken on Trial Island.

work. What can I say except that I am an earthy gal who grew up with a no-frills outhouse. We all use them and appreciate their finer features at home and abroad, so therefore lavatories belong in every sort of literature, including this book. Someday, perhaps someone desperate for a PhD thesis topic will write (if I may humbly suggest a title) "The Toilet in Literature: Refuge and Release." Then my life's work will find its place in the literary firmament at last.

The principal keeper's house was somewhat like the house Jeff lived in on Egg Island, a unique version of the spacious two-storey, four-bedroom farmhouse type with lots of windows and excellent views of both Enterprise Channel and the strait. The actual light tower was mere metres away, a graceful cement structure built in 1970 with a pale green flash for its light. Every single lighthouse and beacon (collectively known as navigational aids) on the West Coast has its own colour of light and its own specifically timed pattern of flashing so that mariners can locate and confirm their own positions on their charts or GPS devices and take action accordingly.

In one of the rare success stories of BC lighthouse heritage preservation, the original Fresnel lens and the cupola were dismantled in 1970 and moved to Victoria's Bastion Square where they are a stationary exhibit, thanks to the BC Maritime Museum. Far too many other decommissioned lighthouses were bulldozed over the nearest cliff or burned to the ground, thanks to those bureaucrats who made such decisions during the eras when Canadian heritage was a misunderstood and even suspect concept. It's still an uphill battle to get any government department to fork out dollars for preservation, as anyone who has hiked by the deteriorating Pachena Point heritage lighthouse with its original Fresnel lens can attest. It was beautiful enough for a Canadian stamp but there has to be political will and a commensurate budget in order to pay for the extensive cost of repairs and upkeep. It's difficult enough for small island communities to rally around their local historic lighthouses with bake sales, let alone protect one quite literally in the middle of such true wilderness as the West Coast Trail. Meanwhile the lightkeepers mop the heritage hardwood floors often, floors that housed a school during the World War II era and hosted many dancing feet of an evening as well.

Trial Island's first lighthouse was built after a series of gruesome marine mishaps, including one poor man drowning because he was trapped by a line around his ankle on board a wreck in a rising tide, a hellish fate the other survivors on land could not spare him from without drowning themselves in the rough seas between them and the wreck. A beacon was built in the early 1900s but the amount of commercial traffic demanded more round-the-clock vigilance. The first lightkeeper, Harrold Shorrock O'Kell, arrived in August of 1907. He was a hardy young sailor with a cork peg leg, due to a nasty accident at sea involving a snapped cable.

The island's very name, I discovered, came from BC's early colonial days when British ships would put in at the dry docks in Esquimalt for a refit. Then the shipwright and crew would take the vessel out a few nautical miles to the islands offshore, checking the re-caulked seams and tightening the rigging en route, before turning back and heading to Esquimalt Harbour again. These trial runs led to the name: Trial Islands.

After Jeff showed me his house, we walked around the main island and talked and talked. I heard more voices. Too many voices, in fact, and music: light rock and pop tunes as well. Jeff smiled at my astonishment, having kept this little surprise to himself. There, smack in the middle of Trial Island, were four tall Meccano-style radio towers I hadn't paid any attention to on the boat ride, one rising from a rectangular shed. Within this shed blared the upbeat baritone of a DJ and highly danceable music courtesy of CFAX Radio. We danced among the grassy hummocks to Steve Miller's "Space Cowboy" and then carried on more sedately with our walk. It was a low-profile rocky island except for plentiful dead grasses, dried-out shrubs and nature's own bonsai versions of Garry oaks.

My ears picked up the downshifting of truck gears and emergency vehicle sirens from the city of Victoria. We could see tiny golfers on the Uplands Golf Course and the glint of vehicle windshields on Beach Drive. People were walking their dogs on McNeill Bay Beach. We both waved, feeling slightly silly, in case my friend Lorna was over there walking Jet, her lovely black dog. There were, in fact, a good number of glossy, energetic black dogs on the beach that day. So we waved and it became a little ritual as we walked around the barren island thereafter, to stop and wave at the dogs and their humans across the channel.

I could see how swift and swirly the currents between Lesser Trial Island

and the big island were and we watched skillful kayakers testing their mettle in sleek sea kayaks and some of the short, agile river kayaks I'd first seen in a river slalom race in North Wales. It wasn't exactly the place to launch my fifteen-year-old plastic sea kayak with its foot-controlled rudder, beamy width and plenty of hollow compartments to accommodate camping supplies. I had only paddled on the ocean in calm conditions thus far and had never had instruction in surf launching or landings. But I'd logged many hours on Slocan Lake for eight years and contended with high, rough waves more than a few times. Paddling on the ocean was a whole new world awaiting.

I was also very conscious of the fact that Victoria's sewage bubbled and churned its way around these islands and out to Juan de Fuca Strait. If my kayak ever flipped, I'd need to stifle the urge to yell open-mouthed for help and wave frantically instead. Then the tweedy geezers in Oak Bay who have their binoculars trained on Trial Island to make sure the flag for Queen and Country goes up at sunrise and comes down at sunset would have to call the authorities to report "some foolish gel out waving in the water or, quite possibly, drowning. Say wot?"

We walked on, slowly, as it wasn't a big island at all, and Woodycat followed us most of the way, yowling in protest if we got too far ahead of him and then rejoining us by taking strategic shortcuts. He was always a "cog": half-cat, half-dog. We could see where the pack of river otters slithered in and out of the water near the remains of a boathouse in a shallow, sheltered little bay. The fishy odour of their dark, greasy calling cards hung in the air. We also kept a sharp eye out for the slimy, pale grey-green turds left by the resident Canada geese. Excrement aside, it was the most sheltered spot to launch our kayaks and possibly even store them, after some bolstering of the old boathouse. I reminded myself that our national goose nested here, along with cormorants and oystercatchers, and that the Trial Islands were part of the Victoria Harbour Migratory Bird Sanctuary. Accept their turds, in other words. Just step lightly and smartly among them. Good advice for all manner of turds, come to think of it.

The large garden plot beside Jeff's house had soil that felt and looked surprisingly promising as well, a nice sandy loam. There were two old compost bins, signs of former gardening activity, but no sign of garden hose stands for watering. Beside the back door was a large plastic tank for runoff water from the roof. The other buildings on site didn't have down pipes or barrels, much less tanks, to catch the winter rain.

For household water, there was a 22,000-litre cistern in the basement with several sets of filters, including a UV filter, and a specified amount of chlorine bleach that needed to be added to the cistern so the water would be safe to drink. All the water supplies for lightkeepers' houses are rigorously tested at least twice annually to make sure that bird droppings, dead rodents and other horrors do not infect the drinking water. Some stations have non-potable water for gardening and fire suppression kept separately in large external cisterns or tanks, and even that water gets a chlorine dose and is monitored twice annually.

Existing in a unique microclimate, Trial Island Lightstation is the driest of all twenty-seven staffed lightstations (followed by the Entrance, Chrome and Merry Island stations), which has led to the island's protected status as part of the Trial Islands Ecological Reserve, comprising twenty-three hectares on Trial, Lesser Trial and several islets. It is an endangered and rare plant sanctuary. Difficult as it was to appreciate this fact on a November day, I looked forward to spring and seeing some of the plants in full flower.

The reserve supports more species of rare vascular (sap-carrying) plants than any known area of comparable size in the entire province of British Columbia. This means it has great value as a seed bank for such plants as the seaside bird's foot lotus, golden paintbrush, rosy owl-clover and white-top aster. Historically, these islands were set afire very carefully by First Nations people who knew that the burning away of late summer grasses would encourage the growth of great and common camas (lilies). They would dig up the bulbs, a staple food in the diet of the Coast Salish peoples, which were usually steamed for twenty-four hours in large covered pits. Said to resemble baked pears, they were so tasty and mildly sweet that they were used alone as well as to augment other foods. They were also sun-dried and pressed into cakes like small bricks after cooking for winter food supplies.

The beautiful blue meadows of camas lilies were, like the salmon-bearing streams, designated to certain families to maintain and harvest and the rights to use them could be passed on to others. With this method of perennial agriculture, of course, people were careful to only harvest larger bulbs, leaving the smaller ones to continue growing. Some years were allowed to elapse before the same island was harvested again so as not to overuse the food source. Not for the first time, I contrasted this ancient sustainable method of permaculture with the herbicide- and fungicide-soaked, chemically fertilized, genetically modified agribusiness methods that have depleted so much prime North American topsoil and polluted rivers and lakes in less than one century.

I took soil samples from the large garden plot beside Jeff's house and sent them off to a lab for testing as there didn't seem to be specific information on the station about heavy metals or toxic materials in that particular spot. They tested for everything from aluminum to mercury to zinc, with the unholy trio of arsenic, cadmium and lead being my main concern. The lab got back to me within ten days. Happily, the soil passed all the tests with absolutely no red flags waving. We were good to grow.

Two weeks later, I was back for another weekend visit on Trial Island. I quickly planted six cloves from a bulb of elephant garlic I'd brought over and made a list of seeds to bring in for spring planting. The station didn't have a greenhouse—a rarity as most lightstations do have at least one—but there was verified good soil, uncontaminated by a century of lead paint or mercury spills from old Fresnel lens systems, or from any other toxic garbage dumped unceremoniously by early keepers and work crews.

The industrious first keeper at Trial, Harrold Shorrock O'Kell, maintained the light and raised a family there for more than a quarter of a century. Needing fresh milk for their baby, Mr. O'Kell arranged to buy a cow in Oak Bay, built a raft, secured the poor beast with ropes around her horns and towed the raft behind his rowboat to bring the cow safely across Enterprise Channel (surely at slack tide) to Trial Island. No word on whether a bull was brought over or whether the poor bovine had to endure a round trip annually in order to be bred to keep producing calves and milk.

The soil in the large plot beside the assistant's house came from O'Kell's twenty-five years of rowing over to Oak Bay, shovelling soil into pails and sacks, and bringing it back to Trial Island to spread into containers and onto plots for flowers and vegetables. It was also said that the O'Kell family rowed over to Oak Bay to have a weekly bath in order to conserve water during the summer. The stringent collection of rainwater from the roofs and recycling of dishwater into the flower beds and main garden transformed the lightkeeper's grounds into a blooming and productive paradise. I'm sure the milk cow's manure was put to good use in the gardens as well.

Today, there is a large flat lawn, which may have once been a potato patch and before that a camas lily meadow, that serves as a helicopter landing pad. Hardy orange calendulas and purple irises still bring welcome splashes of seasonal colour in borders around both houses. I wondered how long these plants had lived on Trial and of course, as on every lightstation I've visited and worked on since, I wondered who planted which perennial plants, a lasting legacy maintained by attentive pruning, mulching and watering by succeeding keepers.

At this point, the Careful Gardener-Reader will have come to the correct conclusion: the enthusiastic assistant lightkeeper's wife still doesn't understand the situation about the availability of fresh water and her ambitious future gardening plans. Also, that this island, so close to a major urban centre and so relatively easy to get out to, is not about to be renamed Serendipity Isle any time soon. We realized we'd made an expedient decision. We'd settled for convenience and proximity, and good as it was for me to be able to visit every two or three weeks for a whole weekend, it just wasn't a very adventurous or truly wild spot.

Jeff and I had one last feast together and then I had to hope for calm seas to leave the next morning, back to the parallel universe of my own workaday reality. Still, we tried to cheer each other up—there was Christmas on Trial to look forward to.

Four weeks later, Seamus and I flew in a helicopter from the Shoal Point base in Victoria to Trial Island, a short ten-minute hop. The Original Family Trio was reunited and Seamus enjoyed the novelty of his first visit to a real lighthouse, especially when a whopper of a winter storm moved in. Winds of over 100 kilometres an hour pushed between the window panes and the high-pitched shrieking of this compressed and funnelled wind kept us all awake the first night. Early the next morning, Jeff started work on resealing the windows. The storm and its near-hurricane-force winds raged on. Towering walls of green sea water frothed all around the island and even the gulls stopped flying. It was exhilarating, in a word.

An experienced assistant keeper from Pachena Point Lightstation had come in to replace the principal keeper on Trial Island to allow for a family Christmas off the lights. There was a pervasive sense of lightness and celebration with no tedious work projects to bog down our festive mood. The storm passed and Enterprise Channel settled down enough for friends of our new principal keeper to make the journey across in their kayaks on Boxing Day. We all helped lug their kayaks and gear to higher ground.

Feasts, charades, Pictionary and other games ensued at get-togethers with the other household full of people. It was a wonderful break in routine, an all-too-short week, but in our little house we enjoyed marathon games of Rummikub, a nautical jigsaw puzzle and The Farming Game, our favourite board game. We listened to our recording of Dylan Thomas reading *A Child's Christmas in Wales* and Seamus was pleased to finally grasp, even though we had listened to the wonderful Welsh voice nearly every Christmas, that Thomas really was his great-great-uncle. Long-distance phone calls to our living and breathing families in Manitoba and BC had to suffice this year.

Seamus had returned to Vancouver Island just before Christmas. He was staying with me in the seaside Union Bay cottage while he looked for work, for which he was already drafting job applications. Jeff and he pored over potential employer websites and I proofread his covering letters. Seamus was thinking of the spring and summer ahead too, planning to sail out to Trial on his catamaran with his friend Eric by launching from Cadboro Bay. Except for the two shifts of daily weather reports and routine, eternal vigilance watching the water for any sign of boats in trouble, the keepers were able to enjoy their holiday time with family and friends.

Then our lives returned to "normal." Jeff and I were not very happy about that reality at all. Words like *despair* and *fatigue* come to mind. Work had become a four-letter word for us both, something to be endured between visits.

Here we were, in our late middle-aged phase of life when most people are

Seamus and Caroline on Trial Island, Christmas 2007. Winds gusted over sixty knots during this storm.

at the pinnacle of their chosen careers. We, on the other hand, were feeling trapped and powerless. It's a tough emotional process, starting over, again and again, at the bottom of a new workplace ladder. This is the B-side of leaping from job to adventure to job. All a sensible person can do is put in a stellar performance, no matter what kind of work it is, and take the high road in all ways.

But the future loomed large before us. We simply had to make another move.

SEVEN

Haiku: Decisions

faint hoarse cries float down
the Brant geese are flying south
am I here next year?

Pros & Cons,
Cons & Pros

MONTHS DRAGGED BY, WITH THE DAYS AND WEEKS AKIN TO US BOTH running in wet cement two hundred kilometres apart from each other, albeit in touch daily by email or phone. Jeff decided to apply for another available position, knowing he stood a snowball's proverbial mortality in Hades of getting it as he had less than a year's work experience on two stations. But that wasn't really the point. It was the only polite and professional means of letting the powers-that-be know that he wanted off the particular rock he was on, sooner rather than later.

Meanwhile I wrote another bird poem, a new addition to the suite of poems using Japanese forms I had begun on Egg Island. Before then I hadn't written much more than a grocery list for many months but now, any time I visited Jeff, I was beside Big Ocean, under Big Sky. I was freed up to write beyond my one or two precious Saturdays a month spent in public libraries toiling on my Peace River *Odyssey* novel, now titled *Penny Loves Wade, Wade Loves Penny*, which I had begun in 1995. (The early working title, ironically, was *The Long Haul*.) Or else I'd be tinkering with yet another version of the children's picture book, *Singing Away the Dark*, which had been verbally accepted back in October of 2006. I had yet another book simmering on the back burner, but it couldn't make up its mind as to whether it was a picture book or a chapter book for young readers. I'd started that one on January 1, 1999, and kept its working title, my homage to the West Kootenay villagers in New Denver and Silverton, *The Village of Many Hats*.

My book-writing life was on hold, however, while I waited for actual interest, not to mention palatable and legally binding contracts to arrive from assorted publishers. Then I waited for other people's maternity leaves and book projects and world travels to end so they could apply their professional skills to my books, instead of their own, as a priority. For an impatient person like me, waiting for other people is truly hellish. I meet every single deadline and have done so since working as a high school weekly columnist for the *Alaska Highway News*. I would perish in a heap of human hyperventilation rather than miss a deadline.

From my scribbled daybook notes while on Trial Island I have the following trenchant words: "Cormorants are the undertakers / spectral dense black observant slow to move / waiting in trios and quartets / at Death's watery door."

A far cry from the poems celebrating pigeon guillemots and oystercatchers I wrote while on Egg Island. Our wilderness island dreams for a future together were crumbling.

Then Jeff called me one cold and rainy April day in 2008 to tell me he'd nearly fallen to the ground to hug the knees of the supervisor who discreetly asked him if he was interested in the assistant's lightkeeper's position on Lennard Island.

Jeff is a moderate and quiet sort of prairie guy so he managed to repress spontaneous tears of sheer relief.

"Yes! I would really like that!" he yelped as softly as is possible to yelp.

Then he was asked if he could fill in for the principal keeper at Entrance Island Lightstation near Nanaimo for several weeks, starting soon.

"Oh, yes, I would really like that, too," he exhaled as quietly as he could.

That did it for me. I had always enjoyed my publishing work blitzes in Tofino and Ucluelet, on the coast near Lennard Island, and there were some good writers who lived there too, not to mention more fantastic restaurants per capita than any other small BC villages I could think of. A number of popular cookbooks I carted around by the box load contained recipes and mouth-watering photographs of the work of notable local chefs. I rediscovered *The Lighthouse Cookbook* by Anita Stewart, a classic smorgasbord of BC lighthouse history and inspired recipes collected from BC lightkeepers. I devoured it. Lennard Island was the only lightstation she didn't visit, due to the treacherous ramp one was expected to land on after nimbly leaping off a boat, and she didn't trust herself to manage it—an able-bodied seaman had recently leapt and spread-eagled himself upon the chilly waters right beside the steep and slimy ramp. Nonetheless, Margaret and Tony Holland, lightkeepers on Lennard from 1974 to 1996, had contributed their family's favourite oatmeal cookie recipe to the collection via Canada Post.

Lennard Island here we come! I vowed to leave my job in order to become a full-time writer again. It was my last chance to really go for it, as I knew I would never be able to "retire" and then commence spritely storytelling. Life is short and precious and I was not put on this earth to sell everyone else's books forever. I would also see if I might suit the position of relief lightkeeper for a few weeks or months a year.

Lennard Island Lightstation is situated at the mouth of Clayoquot Sound, its white light flashing every ten seconds since 1904. From 1906 until 2003, a booming foghorn also warned mariners away from the jagged reefs and rocks. There is a large lawn with two circles of bleached mussel shells visible in even the thickest fog, which serves as the helipad. Lennard Lightstation is also smack in the middle of a group of six lightstations in southwest Vancouver Island, so that meant fairly frequent helicopter flights overhead, and potentially more opportunities to get in and out to Victoria. There was a long-established Coast Guard Lifeboat Station in Tofino itself, three nautical miles away, and their Zodiac 753 lifeboat would be the main means of transportation for Lennard's lightkeepers and for mail pickup and delivery as well.

Tofino had a medical clinic with three doctors, a community hospital and an airport for smaller planes bound for Vancouver's South Terminal and elsewhere on Vancouver Island. Ideally situated halfway between Tofino and Ucluelet, the airport accommodated the occasional Learjet for vacationing sports and entertainment celebrities too. There was also the Tofino Bus, a reasonably priced public bus service seven days a week to and from Victoria via Port Alberni and Nanaimo. The credit union had branches in both villages, and each had full-service Co-op stores offering a full range of fresh, frozen, dry and canned groceries, not to mention gumboots, hardware, clothing for the whole family and a gas station too. What else? Veterinary service once a month in the basement of the Tofino Legion, right beside a branch of the

Vancouver Island Regional Library. Chiropractors and massage therapists, naturopaths, liquor stores, post offices—check, check and check!

Jeff was scheduled to move from Trial to Lennard in early June of 2008. I was up to my neck in work as usual, but I knew I had to coordinate moving all our belongings from our rented cottage in Union Bay to the warehouse at Shoal Point Coast Guard Base in Victoria so that a Coast Guard ship could take all our worldly goods on the one allowable trip per family unit up the west coast of Vancouver Island to our new home.

But first I had to bow out tactfully and gracefully from my work and finesse travel plans well underway for a dream kayak trip around Haida Gwaii with three publishing friends, a long-awaited adventure already booked for the last week of July and first week of August. Life became a round of packing several boxes of personal goods daily, making book-ordering appointments and essentially organizing all the major and minor elements of my personal and professional life. You can only imagine how many lists I crammed into my daybook. Listapalooza.

On my way to attend my last publishers' sales conference in Vancouver, I boarded the Duke Point ferry at Nanaimo. Jeff was working on Entrance Island by then and he and I planned to wave to each other when the ferry came close to the island. Entrance was even smaller than Trial and, Jeff reported, it was positively writhing with garter snakes. Sleep was sometimes difficult because dozens of sea lions hauled themselves out on the flat rocks there and proceeded to bellow non-stop for hours! Pros and cons again. I didn't plan to visit Jeff there as he was only working on the station for two or three weeks at most. I was also secretly relieved. I have a serious snake phobia.

It was a raw and sullen spring day with icy raindrops plopping down. Not another soul was out on the upper deck of the ferry. I stood at the starboard side of the bow as the low profile of the island and the lighthouse tower hove into view. I spotted Jeff running for the shoreline closest to where the ferry would pass. He had the long lens on the camera and while I stood and waved, he waved back and took photos of me waving at him. I burst into tears and waved madly at the tiny waving figure on the rocky shore of Entrance Island until I couldn't see him anymore. God knows what anyone else on board thought we were up to. I cried and cried out there in the cold rain. Despite our sporadic and joyful visits, I was still deeply lonely.

Then I attended the sales conference, a bum-numbing seven-day marathon of listening to presentations and note-taking for several thousand upcoming books. And eating chocolates sent around mid-afternoon to keep our flagging energy levels up and drinking copious quantities of wine at compulsory parties and going out for lovely dinners in Vancouver's better beaneries at day's end with visiting editors and publishers. Well, somebody had to do this job!

I would really miss learning about brilliant new books and getting together with so many witty and lively colleagues, all the fun stuff, without a doubt. I would miss my own book buyers too, a really special, smart and tough bunch of islanders and north coast booksellers who survived despite the relentless loss leader tactics of those who treat books like mass-produced loaves of bread and feckless, fickle consumers who want everything for free, or dirt cheap at least. Let those who know the price of everything and the value of nothing feast on unedited e-books.

I mustered my energy and got through all the final presentations to booksellers and librarians, my resignation speech to Kate Walker, my very understanding friend and employer, and the awful task of packing, thanks to Jeff who came home to pitch in for several crucial days.

The Saturday after my last Friday of work, three friends and I flew as a group from Vancouver to Sandspit on Haida Gwaii. I began making notes for a travel article about kayaking with my adventurous friends, heading out daily in kayaks from our mother ship, the *Anvil Cove*, a sixteen-metre motorized schooner. We explored ancient Haida village sites with Haida Watchmen guides—elders, young carvers, scholars, weavers, women and men. Humpback whales, long-nosed black bears, Sitka black-tailed deer, sooty shearwaters, rhinoceros auklets and northern phalaropes were highlights in wildlife viewing. Skipper Keith Rowsell and cook David Hughes kept us entertained, safe and filled with delicious meals, often using freshly caught seafood. I read two excellent books in my *Anvil Cove* bunk until the small hours, my headlamp shining on the pages of *The Golden Spruce* by John Vaillant, largely set on Haida Gwaii, and then *We Keep a Light* by Evelyn

Richardson, set on Bon Portage Island off the south coast of Nova Scotia, where the author and her family tended the lighthouse for years. Both books won the Governor General's Award for non-fiction in their respective years.

We kayaked for eight days in near-perfect weather around Gwaii Haanas National Park, as far as the UNESCO village site of Skun'gwaii (Red Cod Island Town in translation from the Haida), once known as Nans Sedins or Ninstints, on Anthony Island. I had a new waterproof digital camera but nothing, no words and certainly not me and my rinky-dink little camera, could do justice to the place, with its silvered totem poles leaning or lying at rest, returning to the earth. There is a presence there that is ancient, enduring and spiritually profound.

Back on land, in a mighty Impala procured from Rustic Rentals, we set off exploring Old Masset, Tlell, Skidegate and Queen Charlotte City for another five days. We treated ourselves to a superb eight-course Haida feast made by chef Roberta Keenawii Olsen in her home kitchen, where Jeff and I had our own official wedding dinner in 2006. I cannot recommend this lovely chef or her land and sea feasts highly enough.

This adventure with Karen Stacey of Hornblower Books in Quebec and Paddy Laidley and Sandy Cooper of Raincoast Books in BC turned out to be my retirement present to myself. I will never forget the Book Ladies, as one local fellow called us when issuing a party invitation. There we were in our best nautical/safari outfits, clanking up the gangplank to our mother ship, loaded down with bottles of wine for the seafaring days ahead. (A girl could end up shipwrecked on Gilligan's Island North, after all.) We learned so much and laughed so much. I hereby vow to take them to the lavender fields of France when I win the lottery or write an international bestseller, whichever comes first. There we will bicycle with nothing heavier than a baguette in our picturesque bike baskets, wobbling from inn to château to bistro, to eat, drink and sleep like very content and footloose Book Ladies indeed.

But as for me and my dreams of a big travel article sale, Haida Gwaii turned out to be the sort of destination that associate editors of Canadian magazines and newspapers wrote about while on their own summer holidays, so they had no interest in a little-known BC writer's offerings. My decades-old travel writing sales to the *Alaska Highway News*, *Miss Chatelaine* (yes), *Ski Trax* and *Western Living* more recently meant little in this new era of blogs. The pay per line inch from major newspapers was now much less than I'd been paid in the sixties and seventies by magazines and small-town newspapers. I knew I had to kick-start my own writing career in real and virtual isolation, and I was desperate to make it happen.

It was now or never. Mind you, all it takes is relentless hard work, belief in one's own talent despite worldly indifference to any such notion for years on end, a few discerning publishers willing to take a chance on you and a lightning bolt of impeccable timing combined with sheer dumb luck. Piece of cake, really. Anyone with access to the alphabet can write a book. Apparently. But on the up side, my notes about my Haida Gwaii adventure have found their way into the fourth draft of a 327-page manuscript tentatively called *The Rising: First Voyage of the Seafaring Lady*, a book for teens set in 2060, which needs another draft or three.

Then, on my own again in Union Bay, I dealt with a dishonest pair of creeps from a moving company, followed by a lying carpet cleaner who didn't show up, finding someone else who did with only a few hours' notice and giving him a bottle of leftover sales conference champagne and a twenty-dollar tip, selling my trusty little Chev Tracker to a nice lady barber from Port Alberni, and managing a two-weekend garage sale with only one major back spasm attack, attended with perfect timing by my lovely massage therapist, Jan Shields, and her therapist friend visiting from Quebec.

Imagine me groaning, supine on a cardboard box hastily flattened and slapped down on the cement floor of the carport, while two registered massage therapists worked over my agonized muscles. It was a gift in all ways. I got through it and vowed I would not move my household again for at least a decade. Each move we'd made was more hellacious than the last.

Life was so much simpler when I lived by myself. If stuff didn't fit into my van, I sold it or gave it away. And off I would go again with a lighter load of my essentials. This time, since Seamus was now living in a tiny rental apartment and working as a sailboat rigger in Sidney, we had to take all his boxes of Lego and his railway tracks and boxes of books from Beatrix Potter through *Swallows and Amazons*, his baby clothes (okay, that was me, hanging on to them for future grandchildren) and heaven knows what else. I drew the line

at his labour-intensive, to-scale thatched-roof replica of Shakespeare's Globe Theatre and it was dismantled. Someday he will have a house somewhere and when he least expects it, his father and I will sneak up in the middle of the night and leave a large pile of strangely familiar boxes in his driveway and sneak off again.

When all our stuff was trucked down to the Coast Guard dock in Victoria, I drove Jeff's car, a small but valiant Toyota Echo stuffed to the gills with fragile plants and paintings and glass and pottery, over the mountain highway to Tofino. The Coast Guard lifeboat crew, bless them all, helped me move this final load of precious household crap into their Zodiac and away we went.

Twenty minutes later, on August 15, 2008, I leapt onto the ramp, nice and dry at slack tide, with my computer bag in my grasp. The rest went up the high line in a big white bag called a bonnet. Jeff grinned non-stop and said, "Welcome home."

It had been fourteen long months of separation but now everything was perfect. We could finally live together again and I could start writing in this watery wilderness—once my left eye stopped twitching and my back stopped hurting, of course. I've lost track of how many drafts of my books have been written while standing and typing at a kitchen counter because I could not handle sitting in any kind of chair.

Lennard Island was a mini-paradise: a mature spruce grove offered a buffer from northeast winds, terraces and borders were filled with daisies, dahlias, crocosmia, phlox, lupins and other flowers (and hundreds of snowdrops, daffodils, scilla and Lily of the Nile come spring, a glorious sight). There was a pond with ivory-pink lilies floating on it, surrounded by astilbe, irises and more Shasta daisies. Red-enamelled handrails ran beside a cement "land bridge" at least one hundred metres in length and more than six metres above ground at the apex. The bridge led from the boathouse deck all the way across the island to the radio room. From this scenic view-path, I looked down on a greenhouse and garden beds jammed with foliage.

Sling op: a helicopter carries some of our belongings onto the station, including our two kayaks.

Then Jeff and I walked up to the tall lighthouse tower itself and opened the door. Sixty-seven spiral stairway steps and a steep metal ladder led up to the glassed-in cupola and a 360-degree walkway with red handrails around it, and views of the Esowista Peninsula and Tofino at the tip, the Nuu-chah-nulth village of Opitsaht and Wickaninnish, Frank, Tonquin, Felice, Clayoquot and Vargas Islands. We stared from all 360 degrees as we walked around the cupola of the tower. Our new home, Clayoquot Sound, was wild and stunningly beautiful.

Did I mention Lennard Island has no snakes? Or rodents, bears, wolves or cougars? Unless the latter two carnivores swim over... which wolves and cougars are both very capable of doing, as are deer. It has slugs, however, millions of them bent on devouring my garden greens, the B-side of no natural predators (in this case, garter snakes). I could live with that problem.

The very next morning, when Jeff was out working and the house was quiet except for the sounds of Woodycat crunching his way through his breakfast kibble, I made notes in my daybook. Lists of ideas, of plans, possibilities... as to which articles and stories and poems I would commit to working on in the month ahead. Bliss. Bliss and then a barbecue on the boat deck with the principal lightkeeper, newly arrived from Quatsino Lightstation where he'd been the assistant keeper, and his visiting wife, a full-time elementary school librarian on the BC mainland. Somewhere out there beyond our horizon was Hawaii and then Japan. We toasted both island nations and our own. I could hardly wait to start writing.

As if. Best-laid plans et cetera. On August 25, a mere ten days after my arrival, Jeff was called away to work on Trial Island as the acting principal keeper and I stepped into Jeff's shoes for my first stint as the acting assistant keeper on Lennard Island.

But first, of course, I'd made yet another kind of list, one that I hoped would inspire me in the days ahead:

1. Learn to play a musical instrument
2. Learn Spanish
3. Become very fit and healthy
4. Become a really good bread baker

5. Write, write, write!
6. Rediscover long-buried flair for visual arts by quilting and painting again
7. Learn to love solitude. Learn to accept and love myself, flaws, virtues and the whole empanada
8. See #7, part 2, and apply to husband
9. Learn to love and appreciate everything about this life
10. Become content. Age gracefully

EIGHT

Chief Engineer's Office,
Department of Marine and Fisheries,
Ottawa, Canada

1st February, 1902

The Agent,
Marine Department,
Victoria, B.C.

Sir,

In reply to yours of the 25th ultimo, I have to advise you that the Department will not supply hot water connections to the bath room at Brockton point light-station.

Hot water in a bath room is considered a luxury, and if keepers desire luxuries they must pay for them themselves.

Brockton Point is the only lighthouse in the Dominion that has a bath room of any kind supplied to it.

(sgd.) Chief, Engineer

Growing Up Under
Wide Skies

I GREW UP WITH A LOT OF FREEDOM AND SOLITUDE IN THE PEACE RIVER wilderness because our homestead at the end of a gravel country road, bordering the breaks of the Beatton River, offered many hectares of it. The breaks, or riverbanks, were deemed non-arable and could be leased for grazing purposes only. There were 130 hectares of coulees, hoodoos, hog's backs, sage, cactus, crocuses, wild cranberries, spruce and poplar trees and silver willows, tough pumpelly brome, altai fescue grass and some hand-seeded alfalfa and clover. A water scoop-out (most people call them dugouts) we'd had excavated by a Caterpillar tractor up on the flat plateau and the lean, brown Beatton River below provided two reliable sources of water for wild and domestic animals.

The vestiges of a pack trail pounded down into the earth of the breaks by thousands of years of Dane-zaa First Nation (formerly Beaver Indian) hunters, the occasional arrowhead, two or three unusual shallow depressions we thought might be graves, and once, a pouch of dried pemmican… all these things stoked my TV-free imagination. Then there were the stories our Welsh father told us about neighbours arriving in the early thirties to find three sets of teepee poles still standing where we now had fields. He also told us about the hunters coming down in the fall to shoot deer at the salt spring near the river and trading fresh venison for his homemade bread and spare tea and tobacco. After World War II, though, the Dane-zaa hunters were confined to the Doig River Reserve far to the north and the visits and trading stopped.

In the spring and right through the summer to the fall, my sister Marion (Mi) and I rode our Percheron-cross workhorses out to check on where our cattle herd was grazing, and to report any fence breakage beyond our fixing abilities and any possibility of missing calves or cows. We constantly checked the ground for animal tracks and we learned to read other signs: carrion birds circling overhead, a normally calm cow bellowing angrily while running along the fence line, her udder distended. We smelled the air for the stench of meat decomposing and we used the binoculars to scan the sage-covered breaks, looking for the gleam of fresh bones and scattered reddish Hereford hair, signs signifying a calf lost and a grieving cow in pain until her milk dried up. True, there was food for a black bear, coyotes too if they were quick, and they usually were, and what was left went to the crows and grey jays.

But it was also much-needed money lost for our family come fall when the cattle would be trucked to Patterson's Auction Barn in Dawson Creek. I never liked to imagine that part of it, the crowding of so many cattle into trucks, then railcars, the dust and confusion, their hunger and thirst, all that before the killing blow. When the cattle trucks drove in I'd go off on a horse or a long walk to cry by myself to avoid the pain of seeing and hearing all the sounds of cow-calf separation. Curbing my imagination was as necessary a skill then as it is now.

Winter meant hauling and splitting wood blocks from the snow-covered woodpile, loading our toboggan with as many blocks as it could carry and tugging it over to our unheated porch, and making another, neater pile there. We only had wood heat, from the kitchen stove and the wood heater in our living room, during the farm years.

But first it meant helping Dad skid out frozen, limbed poplar trees with our team of horses pulling the sleigh runners only, onto which the logs were piled by us, one by one. Later we sawed them with the buzz saw run by the belt between the John Deere tractor and the saw in a marathon day—or worse, two—of cold and heavy work. Poplars burn quickly, unlike dense birch, but we had very little birch on our land.

Winter also meant hauling in tubs of snow to melt on top of the kitchen stove for water, then pouring more snow into the barrel standing beside the stove. The cattle and horses were brought up from grazing on the breaks by then, to join our year-round pair of milk cows in the home pasture. All the animals were fed our good alfalfa hay through the harsh winters and on Christmas Day oats too, if we had enough, in the barnyard.

Summer was a short but intense season of more than twenty hours of daylight daily. We'd be out hoeing, hilling and watering our garden, shelling peas until our thumbs ached, pampering our six-square-metre 4-H Happy Harvester garden plots and racing the impending frost to dig up the thirty-plus rows of potatoes. Then there was the daily chore of feeding and watering the chickens and collecting their eggs.

Mi and I spent endless hot, dusty, scratchy weeks on a stone boat pulled by the John Deere tractor driven by our dad, stacking nine twenty-kilo bales into an alfalfa inukshuk before shouldering the entire pile off the stone boat onto the field for later pickup by the hay rack. We also spent a lot of our childhood arranging thousands of bundles of wheat and oats into stooks, mini-teepees of six or seven individual bundles leaned together to better shed any rain or snow. We shovelled grain into and out of granaries and shovelled manure out of the barn and onto the gardens in early spring. Dad often worked elsewhere during the winter for wages so it was up to Mi and I, as the two oldest, to help Mom keep the farm going. He'd sometimes make it home for the weekends from the logging camp or wherever he was living and working during the week.

In mid-winter, we chopped a hole through the ice daily, sometimes over one metre deep, on the biggest of our five farm scoop-outs, the one closest to our barn. When the ice was so thick I couldn't use the axe anymore, I used the crowbar to punch through the ice, and tried not to lose the precious heavy implement between my damp or frozen mitts when I finally pierced through. Then the dark water smelling of another world, of plants and mud, bubbled up to the wintry surface for the waiting horses and cattle surrounding me, and they would drink in the order of their dominance in the herd, horses before cows always. All these chores, this necessary, hard and much-valued work, shaped my mental and physical being as a child and a teenager.

So when anyone has the colossal nerve, as one lightkeeper's prissy wife did, to tell me that lightkeeping is really Man's Work—well, I've been far too polite to such presumptuous, sexist individuals to date. But I will state here that I had likely done more hours of hard labour by the time I reached fourteen years of age than most contemporary adult Canadian males have done in their entire lives. I also don't feel like a lesser human being for asking someone else to help me roll a loaded fuel barrel upright or to lift a sixty-four-kilo pressure washer up a set of stairs. It's not macho to sustain a back injury; it's behaving stupidly. I'm less than five foot three in ye olde imperial measurement, vertically challenged as my son likes to tease, and I'm resigned to it.

Some people are squeamish about composting toilets, too, and there are a number of them on BC lightstations. They are odourless and sensible systems, however, when properly maintained. My homestead upbringing has served me well as an adventurous traveller and as a lighthouse keeper. When you've grown up with Eaton's and Sears catalogues for toilet paper, you learn to appreciate the simple things, like the wonderful soft green paper wrappings of Japanese oranges in December. (Rest assured, in this century we place a large double-roll order for toilet paper on each monthly grocery list.)

I never thought we were poor when I was a little kid because we had lots of good food and our clothes and hair were always kept clean, even without the benefit of running water. Besides, nearly everyone else in the farming community was in the same boat as far as spare cash and bathroom amenities went. Then came high school and moving into the dormitory in Fort St. John, a place for sixty boys and sixty girls from isolated ranches, reserves, villages, farms and other places in the north too far from a high school bus route.

My allowance for the week, circa 1966–69, was usually between a quarter and fifty cents to buy my own toothpaste, nylons, shampoo, everything. Once I soaked white cotton batten in white toothpaste to plug a cavity in my front tooth, knowing my parents could not afford the dentist. This went on for a few weeks until I was sent to the dentist by my mortified mother, who caught me attempting this ineffectual form of cosmetic dentistry when I was home for a weekend. I found a job working after school twice a week at a nearby greenhouse for eighty-five cents an hour, which helped immensely. I was also a 4-H Happy Stitchers clothing club member, so with my extra skills I revamped second-hand clothes and once, a pair of shiny olive green curtains we found at the dump. I sewed almost all my own miniskirts and unique little dresses. It's amazing what a bit of flair and a big smile will do for old curtains.

At the end of grade nine, the high school awards ceremony was held and I watched as graduating students walked up to the front to receive commendations and scholarships. As the lists were read out, so too were the plans of the students: to study theatre at the Royal Academy of Dramatic Art in England, to pursue a career in medicine or teaching or agriculture. No future writers because no one wanted to be a dead, white Englishman. The way ahead became very clear to me during that assembly in the gym. It was a pivotal moment, a game-changer that galvanized my focus for the remaining years of high school.

But halfway through grade ten, my mother said I had to quit school and go out to clean "town" people's houses. The dormitory fees were too expensive with both me and my younger sister attending at thirty and twenty-five dollars respectively per month. "But I'm on the honour roll," I said, as calmly as I could muster, and asked if she had discussed it with Dad. Silence. This was a trial balloon, I quickly surmised. There were no Nazi bombs falling on our heads and this, surely, was an overreaction on her part. I adamantly refused to re-enact her own life script with her own mother, who had yanked Mom out of Catholic elementary school after grade seven and sent her out to clean houses and do other menial low-paying jobs. Mom told me later how much she wanted to continue going to school but high school cost money and only the boys in the family were sent on to a trade school. Mom was the seventh of eight children. This drudgery went on for years, including the living hell of World War II in occupied Holland, until my mom, who was terrified of heights, climbed up a rope ladder leading from a small boat to the deck of an ocean-going ship in the bombed-out harbour of Rotterdam. Thus she escaped with two suitcases to marry my dad in Canada, where even more hard work on a homestead, but also great adventures, awaited her.

Dad's story is a little easier to bear but it is still dispiriting in that he was offered a scholarship as the "fourth smartest boy in Wales" but, as the son of a Welsh coal miner and second of eight children, it was not financially possible for him to accept. His family couldn't afford the cost of shoes, school uniforms and other necessities for a boarding school. I still have the proud letter from the headmaster to my grandmother. Dad then had to leave high school early despite his fine mind, bound for London to work in a factory making pots and pans where the chemicals used ruined his sense of smell forever. He left that sinus- and mind-numbing job to immigrate to a homestead with his older brother in the Peace River region. When World War II broke out two years later, he joined an Edmonton infantry regiment and five years later he met Mom at a celebratory street dance for Canadian soldiers in Schiedam. After two months of courting, they spent over a year apart, communicating by letter using English and Dutch dictionaries, until her passage by ship to Montreal and train across Canada to BC in 1947.

I have come by my trait of escaping insufferable work and life situations and risking it all for new adventures quite honestly, with these two as my parents. Who then, of course, wanted me to have a secure, well-paid career so as not to suffer anything like their own hard lives. When I was in grade eleven and twelve, I wrote a weekly column and "youth" articles for the *Alaska Highway News*, which provided a welcome bit of extra cash that freed up my folks from giving me an allowance or paying for any of my clothes. I'd applied at the paper thinking it would be good volunteer experience should I decide to become a journalist. I discovered I was being paid by the line inch when the editor asked me, after two months, to bring in my columns so he could measure them. The length of my "School Daze" columns increased exponentially and I was careful to list all the students belonging to all the teams and school clubs and going on major excursions, being very inclusive, which pleased many students and all their parents, as I also made sure everyone's names were spelled correctly. I always made the 4:00 p.m. Wednesday deadline at the AHN, where Ma Murray wheeled around the place ostensibly run by her son Dan.

I came to the early conclusion that nobody else would actually live my one and only life except for me, which is not to say that I didn't attempt my best impersonation of a Good Girl along the way. "To thine own self be true" said Shakespeare, which is great advice, but for most of us, sorting out one's true self can take more than a few years, especially with a distinct lack of knowledgeable guidance as far as writing careers went, never mind career mentors and role models. I knew I could never afford to own a newspaper, for starters.

My goals at the age of fifteen were to keep my own surname like other women writers with gumption did, which branded me as "unnatural" according to at least one idiot. Secondly, I vowed never to be trapped by any possessive boyfriend because thirdly, I had to get a university education and then, somehow, travel the world. All this would need to be accomplished on my own nickel because my folks had three other kids to get through school. So I set about studying hard and won a bunch of scholarships to get to the University of British Columbia in Vancouver. And then, despite having far too much fun, for the first two years especially, I kept up the pace, augmented with full- and part-time jobs, to graduate with a bachelor of arts and then a high school teaching certificate.

After observing my years of effort, my father at last recognized my ambition to be a writer, and bless him, he was in a position to give me enough money to attend David Thompson University Centre for that one crucial year. This was at a time when I was a seasonal gardener and house caretaker on North Pender Island in the Gulf Islands with very little money in my savings account. Apparently Dad said I'd be "all set after my first book"—a validation of my talent and tenacity that I wish he'd told me directly... it took years for me to finally hear about it. It's so sad that we humans retain harsh criticism, emotional acid dumped on our hearts and burned into our brains, so much more than rare and loving praise as we make our way in this life. Thankfully, I have always had the kind of rebellious attitude that reacts fiercely to mean, stupid people. "Oh, yeah? See ya, wouldn't want to be ya! Die soon!" But seriously, the best revenge is always to keep writing, stay healthy and keep laughing. That drives them nuts.

So long to the ditzy amateur fortune-teller in Canada who declared me "too scattered" due to the number of vowels and the configuration of consonants in my good name, which true to my fifteen-year-old self has remained unchanged. Thank you to the quiet Hindu numerologist in Jaffna who sighed and said I would be a seeker of knowledge all my life. Farewell to the famous psychic who said I would only write four books and that I was so good at working with young people that I should do that instead. Well, Madame, you died before my fifth book came out.

Lesson learned: don't hand any power over your own creative life to practitioners of malarkey, even for a lark. I'm not talking about editors and other working professionals, even tin-eared theatre directors must be endured, but the nattering bystanders who are so often failed artists themselves. Nobody is as vicious or as cynical as a wounded idealist or self-proclaimed artist who doesn't work nearly hard enough or take any good advice. Advice to self, and to my Gentle Reader: heed your inner radar and honour your own gutsiness and smarts, and forever love the family and friends who stand by you cheering, despite all your opinionated feistiness and legendary foolishness. Eventually, our minds and bodies let us know exactly when we cannot lie to ourselves and then, if we have sufficient courage and willpower, we will bushwhack our own paths to a meaningful life.

My initial long-term career choices were socially valued, self-sacrificing jobs: teaching, social work and international development endeavours, highly responsible work that was, for me, also a high stress route to burnout. I wanted everyone I worked with to be happy and healthy and firing on all cylinders, but of course even 120-hour work weeks can't guarantee success or perfection. Learning my own fallibility and limitations occupied my twenties and half of my thirties until I became a mother at age thirty-five, a complete game-changer in the focus and energy department.

However, I am slowly and steadily writing and publishing short stories for a collection concerned with altruism, thanks to spending years working in group homes and alternative schools, building roads in Sri Lanka, working with the mentally challenged, the intellectually gifted, the saintly and the slackers. There is always an upside. To this very day, whenever I have to work at anything except writing, I always get through it by telling myself, "This, too, is grist for the writing mill. Keep the nose to the grindstone and the ears and eyes on full alert. Take good notes."

I've read books like I drink water ever since I was six. They've saved my mind and my life. They helped me dream of other places, other worlds, other ways of living. Drudgery and grinding poverty were conquered by others, far worse off than me, and they still enjoyed brave deeds and great adventures. I discovered what many readers do, that I was not alone in this world, that stories connected me to all those resilient, sturdy children, people a lot like me. The fact that most of the action was conducted by people with boys' names or wearing boys' clothes was beside the point. I was Huck Finn on the Mississippi, Black Beauty on the cobbled streets of London and orphan Heidi in the Swiss Alps. Reading allowed me to be any character, human or animal. I was always the one rebellious boy, girl, cat, dog or horse, the one who left the corrupt, class-ridden Old World behind to find the New World by stowing away on a sailing ship. I was never aligned with the obedient, timid types doing needlepoint and filling a hope chest with embroidered linens, waiting for somebody rich enough to come along and make all the key decisions about where and how to live and what to think and whatever shall we do next.

What gave me the place to reflect and to explore my perceptions of the world and myself was the diary I began writing in 1970, the very day after leaving home with my sister, Mi, to work at a garage/café/motel at Mile 146½ on the Alaska Highway. It was excellent writing practice, although much of the early diaries are in a form of code I used to defy the family snoops and a succession of roommates. Many pages are cringe-worthy in any case. None of it will ever see the light of day or the lights above a bookstore shelf, or its digital equivalent. But I would eventually write a story called "Summer Wages" inspired by the short summer season that Mi and I worked there as a waitress and chambermaid, respectively. It is my most anthologized story to date, in collections by Oxford, Prentice-Hall, Nelson Canada and Irwin Publishing, now read in Canadian English classes from high school to the university level.

In my journals, there are kernels of self-awareness and growing wisdom, as well as concise or even interesting descriptions of my travels and the people I've met and worked with, and notes to myself about stories I want to write. So many stories, some of which I have yet to write. There are simply too many of them because choosing writing allows me to be curious about everything... So there are many, many notebooks all packed into waterproof totes in the basement of our lightstation home. Jeff has his totes filled with photographs and negatives, as well as his early chapbooks, story manuscripts and magazine articles.

With Shakespeare's memorable quote flooding my brain cells on a frequent basis, I knew I had maybe three decades left to live, four if I took very good care of myself. I'd been paid for my writing since I was sixteen years old, Girl Reporter on the loose. But my pursuit of knowledge and life experience has rarely been about the paycheque. It's about the richness of the experience, the extent of the adventure, the interesting people and places I might get to know and understand. Jeff and I didn't have any spare money to travel the world together and we were, frankly, too old and our skills too generalized to be of any use in rigorous overseas placements on a volunteer or country-wage basis.

The lightkeeping life was going to be our next Great Adventure, a saner way to make a year-round wage than holding down two or three or more part-time jobs between us, even though lightkeepers are the lowest-paid federal civil servants. But, just as in the old days, the lightstation houses were "free," part of the salary, and the fuel to heat them came with the job as well. These concrete benefits and the fact that keepers work seven days a week would give us a slow but steady way to save money for our eventual retirement. It was time for me to climb the rope ladder, get on the ship and head out to the lighthouse.

NINE

4:25 a.m. First Weather Report Waka

Stars fill the whole sky
The lights of one boat glimmer
Here I stand gazing…
Out to sea and up to sky
This is me on Earth, shining!

A Little Green Rock
to Call Home

WHEN I FIRST TOLD PEOPLE I WAS MOVING OUT TO THE "LIGHTS," their reactions were either shared delight or sheer fright. No in-between emotions or opinions were ever registered.

"Won't you worry about missing… things?" asked one colleague, eyeing me with concern.

"Not at all," I said, "I'll fill my days by doing all the things I actually want to be doing, not what other people want me to do."

Well, this was before I started doing so much relief work that I blew through my ninety days a year allotment as a casual relief worker. I wrote my assistant lightkeeper's exam in order to qualify for unlimited time to work. That does mean doing work other people want me to do but I'm okay with most of that, for now. I do not miss meetings and phone calls and driving many thousands of kilometres for work at all. Or being trapped behind a bookstore counter for hours on end being pleasant and helpful when I'd prefer to be in my ratty old housecoat at my computer. Instead of surreptitiously scribbling plot points on the back of special order slips under the bookstore counter, I'd rather be out here in the rain and fog and wind, clearing my head and developing momentum for a coherent storyline or finding my way to ending a poem.

"The world is full of too many books as it is," commented one jaded book person who didn't know I'd already published four of them. "Do you really want to add to it?"

"Nobody else in this world has my stories," I said, unsmiling, for once able to summon exactly the right reply to a rude remark. She had the decency to look ashamed. I went on to publish three more books in my first four years of living on the lights. The best revenge for naysayers is to live well, write like an energetic angel and ignore dream-squelching assholes as much as possible.

"Will you ever wear clean clothes?" blurted my horrified hairdresser, so adept at blonde streaks and red lowlights and other coiffure *trompe l'oeil*, at what would turn out to be my last appointment with him after seven years.

"Oh, I'll wear coveralls and steel-toed gumboots and a yellow raincoat most of the time," I chortled, giddy as a loon in love. He and his lovely wife operated a hospitable and über-creative hair salon that I still miss, but we shared hardscrabble farm backgrounds.

I actually like wearing old clothes and not fussing about them or my hair until I have to head off to be a Semi-Famous Writer. Then I fuss and fret, like women socialized in the last century tend to do, about what outfit makes me look skinnier or fatter, or worse, dull and matronly, but only for a limited amount of time until I've done my public persona work in some sort of floating black outfit with zippy red shoes. Soon enough I'm back in my lighthouse habitat wearing decrepit T-shirts and nine-year-old baggy jeans with multiple patches. I wear my old clothes until they are worn out completely and then I cut them into rags for the engine room clean rag bin. *Farewell turquoise Proctor Storytelling Festival T-shirt, my fond memories will outlive you.* I save all the zippers and buttons and shoelaces too. Waste not, want not. Or to quote the lightkeeper's mantra upon seeing a floating piece of unidentified material landing on nearby rocks: *That might come in handy some day...*

No one had actually lived in the assistant's house on Lennard for at least a decade. It had been used as an arts and crafts workshop by one of the previous lightkeepers. The walls in the house were a stark flat white and the floors were linoleum, in a pattern of murky brown squares reminiscent of the early seventies when oranges and browns were rampant in home decor and fashion alike.

For ten days we fairly flew around our little red and white Coast Guard house. I washed windows, painted warm adobe-inspired colours over the flat white of the interior rooms and did my best to remove packing tape residue from wooden bookshelves and kitchen chairs and even the washer and dryer.

In the second bedroom, my future writing room, we set up my dad's oak desk. In between coats of paint, I wrote drafts of poems about fog and trees and gratitude. Then I made feast after slow food feast, eight-course curries and cabbage rolls and cinnamon buns. I finally had the time, the expanse of each free day stretching out before me. I embraced my inner Domestic Goddess and gave Her free rein to make Italian sourdough breads and nettle gnocchi.

Jeff worked the early shift. We were on daylight saving time and his alarm rang at 4:00 a.m. so he could do his first weather report at 4:40 a.m. At that hour, I am utterly comatose—I am a ne'er-do-well night owl by nature; noble, virtuous Jeff is an early bird. This was followed by another weather report at 7:40 a.m., by which time I can usually be found upright with both feeble arms outstretched, heading for the coffee pot. Unless the weather took a specific turn for the worse—a wind direction switch in less than fifteen minutes at speeds of more than ten knots, fog rolling in two nautical miles or closer to the station, or waterspouts, all of these potential marine and aviation hazards—his last scheduled weather report was at 10:40 a.m. Jeff unpacked and painted our house as well as mowing lawns and pressure-washing the mould and grime off the station buildings and hundreds of metres of handrails.

Unpacking and settling in to a new and happy life is a much less onerous task than packing up and cleaning and trying to fit everything into a specific number of boxes. My back wobbled a few times, still tender and recovering from the big move, but when it spasmed, I'd immediately get horizontal with ice packs between the floor and my lower lumbar zone, having rubbed in some anti-inflammatory arnica lotion and swallowed an extra-strength heavy-duty Robaxacet if it was really starting to act up. My kind of holistic approach, I guess you could call it: throwing everything available at the ailment in question. I would then attempt to close my eyes and breathe through it, resting my twitching eyeballs, or reading a book to distract myself from the pain of the poison darts some jeering deity was jabbing into me.

Near the top of my list of long-range things I wanted to accomplish while living on the lights was getting fit and healthy again. I was being reminded that my pain-filled, buckling back was my own handy personal stress barometer and I had to take full responsibility for it. I was slowing down and listening. Finally. It seems I need painful refresher courses on stuff like this.

I kept a spare VHF radio near me as I worked in the house so that I knew if a Coast Guard helicopter was coming in, or the lifeboat was bringing mail from Tofino, or if a mayday was transmitted by a mariner or aviator in big trouble. If the lightkeepers on duty were wearing ear protectors as they mowed lawns or weed-whipped or changed the oil in the duty engine, they simply could not hear the radio. When there are only two keepers on the station, this can be an issue, so it's good to have a family member listening, away from the noisy work environment, and then hailing them or sprinting over to wherever they are working if needed.

One August day, Jeff called out on his radio: "Orcas heading north. Lots of them. Boat deck!"

All three of us thundered up to the boat deck with our binoculars and cameras to watch two pods of orcas, at least eighteen in total, one pod heading north at a fast clip and the other smaller group sneaking through our channel and making a getaway. Whale-watching boats from Tofino were already on the scene, their guests leaning over the boat sides with their cameras to capture the photogenic whales going northward. We cheered on the small pod evading the ruckus. Then we all noticed dozens of harbour seals hauled out as high as they could get on the rocky islets and shelves on the reefs surrounding our lagoon. The chubby seals, choice prey for transient orcas, and the bald eagles perched on the flat table rock above were all duly photographed like supermodels wearing fins, fur and feathers. Then it was the turn of the cormorants and oystercatchers who reliably hang out on our reefs to preen for the paparazzi.

Two eagles nested on what we called Lesser Lennard, a small island separated from our much larger one by a deep, narrow gap through which the ocean surged except at the lowest tides. Harlequin ducks and belted kingfishers were regular seasonal visitors too, as well as assorted sparrows, a massive murder of at least one hundred crows, and several ravens that came over to hoot and clunk and creatively clear their throats in order to stir up the crows. Then the trickster ravens snickered away in their hiding spots, hugely enjoying the high-decibel ruckus they'd created. We wished the ravens would set up nests instead of the shrieking crows that plopped their purple salal and blackberry poop or fishy white mess on our handrails.

Crows did a fair bit of damage to our garden seedlings and ripening rasp-berries and blueberries.

Jeff was to train me in weather data collection and reporting before he left for his relief stint on Trial Island, so out I went with him at unnaturally early hours to peer into the darkness, listen to the roar or whisper of the swell and to stare up at the sky. There I might discern the moon and a few stars, or millions of stars, or no moon and no stars whatsoever. Lightkeepers in remote spots, which includes most of us, live and work in a world with very little light pollution from the cities.

Given my childhood on a remote northern homestead, sans electricity until I was twelve years old, I still love just looking at the wide sky at any time, but especially at night. Make that a dry night, with inky darkness, with a heavy-bellied full moon or an elegant fingernail moon, the man-made won-ders of satellites and jets silently soaring far above us, the seasonal rising and fading from view of the planets and major stars with their unearthly hues of blue and red and gold. Most of all, I love seeing the Milky Way undulating across the sky, an infinite shawl of ancient diamonds.

Each morning, we walked to the observation spot on the boat deck to look for the lights of Opitsaht, a village four nautical miles to the north, and the flashing beacon just off Wickaninnish Island two miles to the northwest, both highly visible distance markers, barring fog or heavy rain, storm-caused electrical outage or vandalism to the buoy, all of which has happened during our time on Lennard. The next observation point was on the narrow wooden deck built onto the radio building so off we walked on the cement land bridge connecting the two. Once there, we had an unimpeded view to the southeast and across to the western ocean horizon.

Lightkeepers have the numerically unique situation in that we calculate wind speed in knots, wave and swell height in feet, distance or visibility in nautical miles and precipitation in millimetres. We overhear our Coast Guard ship personnel referring to fathoms and cables, meaning depth and distance, in ye olde nautical measurements as well. Go figure!

Sometimes boats were out on the water, helping Jeff and me gauge just how far we could see by the clarity of their lights or the lack thereof. If their lights were tossing up and down violently, even disappearing from sight on a regular count, it was clear that significant swell action was in the weather mix. Then inside the radio building we went, checking to the east and southeast for the lights of homes on Chesterman Beach one mile away and Frank Island half a mile across Templar Channel between us, and the lodges and resorts on Cox Bay two miles away, Gowlland Rocks four miles hence and the fixed red light five miles away, high on Radar Hill, an aviation marker.

Inside, our focus switched to the anemometer. Wind speed and direction had to be studied for the entire duration of our time in the radio room in order to note any extremes of gusting winds. Unpredictable gusts are hazardous to helicopters, float planes and sailboats in particular. On Lennard, the actual equipment that collected the data for the anemometer was affixed near the top of our lighthouse tower, very sensibly open and accessible to the prevailing winds. Which is to say, our instruments are not situated in the lee of a large building or a dense stand of trees, rendering half of the data nearly useless, as is sometimes the case elsewhere, unfortunately.

There was much to learn but it was interesting stuff so I trotted along listening and jotting notes into my little black Moleskin book, a compulsive habit I've thanked myself for since. I had to integrate the concept of "estimate" and abandon "absolute accuracy" for starters. We lightkeepers have to offer our best estimates as to wave and swell height based on what we observe and the strength of the wind, calculating one foot of wave height for every five knots of wind, especially if we can't see clearly. In the light of day, we can see the ocean surface and estimate fairly accurately the wave height and swell by observing the number and pattern of whitecaps on the waves and the splash heights of the swell on key markers like cliffs and rocks, and by calculating the depths to which a fishing boat hull is obscured when it dips between big swells, or by seeing flat, placid salt water all the way to the unruffled horizon.

In the years ahead of me I would learn how each station is different: some have more data collection tasks and more, fewer or different instruments, but all come with distinct geographic markers—beacons, buoys and distinct land masses or settlements used to assess visibility, and mountains against which to check cloud levels at known altitudes. There are different agencies to collect data for, to record in station record books or to log into our computers in order to send off to Environment Canada. Almost all lightkeepers participate

A sea lion surfs off Egg Island Lightstation.

Aerial shot of Lennard Island Lightstation looking north.

The view from the walk outside the cupola of the Lennard Island tower.

This is Fogust. Hollyhock beaded with moisture and Lennard Island tower in the background.

Tofino lifeboat *Cape Ann* during exercises in a big swell in Cox Bay.

Caroline stands inside the double bull's eye Fresnel lens in the original tower at Pachena Point Lightstation.

Caroline pressure-washes the tank farm at Estevan Point Lightstation.

Caroline takes readings from the thermometers in the Stevenson screen during a brilliant sunset at Nootka Lightstation.

The welcoming figure carved by Sanford Williams and two apprentices at Yuquot faces the open Pacific Ocean.

Caroline's gingerbread people, the product of the annual Christmas bake-a-thon that ends up in gift boxes for CCG (Canada Coast Guard) pilots and engineers, lifeboat crew, local MCTS (Marine Communication and Traffic Services) staff and Victoria's LSO (Lightstation Services Operations) office staff. *Photo by Caroline Woodward*

Snow for the first Christmas on Lennard Island.

Sunrise on Lennard Island.

Caroline begins dill pickle production in the kitchen on Lennard Island Lightstation.

Bigg's Killer Whale T41A and her calf T41A2 swim through the channel between Lennard Island and the reef in the summer of 2011.

The yard on Lennard Island in the summer of 2014 with Jeff and Caroline's house in the background left and the garden shed in the background right.

Selfie of Jeff and Caroline during a relief stint on Quatsino Lightstation, fall 2014.

in the COOLTAP (Co-operative Online Temperature and Precipitation Entry System) program twice daily as weather watch volunteers. About half of the BC lightkeepers collect a sea sample at one high tide daily and measure its salinity and temperature, providing invaluable information for the fisheries and other scientists watching ocean temperatures.

Twice daily we checked the precipitation gauges to see exactly how much rain, snow, ice pellets and/or hail had come down. And we opened the north-facing door of the free-standing white louvred (slatted) box on stilts, a.k.a. our Stevenson screen, to check two thermometers for maximum and minimum daily temperatures. At some stations, there are also wet and dry humidity or dew point measuring instruments called hygrometers. The Stevenson screen is designed to create a standardized environment and to protect the interior from direct sunlight, precipitation, drifting leaves, animal damage, high winds or anything else that could interfere with the data. Your eyeballs have either glazed over by this point or, like me, you actually like becoming a weather nerd.

The screen was invented by the Scottish engineer, lighthouse builder and meteorologist Sir Thomas Stevenson, the father of author Robert Louis Stevenson (*Treasure Island, Kidnapped, The Strange Case of Dr. Jekyll and Mr. Hyde*). Scottish writer Bella Bathurst has written a wonderful biography of this engineering family, *The Lighthouse Stevensons*, which tells how four generations of them built every lighthouse around Scotland and were responsible for a slew of inventions in both construction and optics, including the refining of the Fresnel lens for lighthouse use. The Stevensons and their crews of skilled tradesmen achieved feats of engineering in North Sea conditions that would be utterly forbidding even today using no cordless DEWALT power tools whatsoever.

The next step in the weather reporting process was for us to stand by the ALN (Automated Lighthouse Network) circuit and its heavy black phone, which looks like something out of the 1970s and to which each circuit of lightstations is connected. Lennard was on the same circuit as the Carmanah Point, Pachena Point, Cape Beale, Estevan Point and Nootka lightstations. With Jeff the Taskmaster close by, I practised delivering my weather report in a clear and measured cadence because the data collectors from Marine Communications and Traffic Services (MCTS) would be simultaneously entering our data into their computers. But first I had to write it all in our lightkeeper's log as follows:

CLDY 15 SE11 2'CHP LSW OCNL RW-

Meaning Lennard's sky is cloudy, with more than five-eighths of the dome above us covered in clouds. I say aloud the double numbers as individual digits—i.e., I can see fifteen miles, so the visibility is one-five nautical miles or more to the sea's horizon. The winds are from the southeast with an average eleven (one-one) knots of speed. Wave height is estimated at a two-foot-high chop with a low (one- to six-foot-high) swell coming in from the southwest. In remarks, I state occasional (OCNL) light rain showers (RW-).

In the ensuing years, I've learned how important the weather observations and reports provided by lightkeepers are to the public. The business of commercial and sports fishing, towing loads along the coast, taking paying guests out to see and photograph wildlife, flying safely from point A to point B and guiding safe kayaking excursions all depend on up-to-date local weather reports. Although nearly everyone on the water also checks the major offshore buoy readings and the Pacific marine forecast for their region on the internet, our observations flow into the continuous marine broadcast on VHF radios and the Environment Canada website daily. If anyone is out on the water in BC and would like a local weather report from a lightkeeper, they can hail the nearest one of us at 82 Alpha, our working channel, on VHF.

Mariners planning long voyages up the coast or fishing boats wanting to cross Queen Charlotte Sound and other notorious stretches usually have a Global Positioning System (GPS) on board but (a) GPS and its satellite technology can malfunction, yes indeed, a real shock for those who revere technology, but it can and does fail and never at the right time and (b) we still hear people on channel 16, the distress channel, who do not know how to use a functioning GPS getting into big trouble. Lightkeepers can relay accurate weather information from other lightstations farther up or down the coast thanks to our ALN connection. We give mariners and aviators current on-site information as to whether conditions are good or bad, or a heads-up that a big storm we've been expecting has actually come in early or fizzled.

I'll never forget one Southern Straits race that Seamus participated in that resulted in a monohull sailboat capsizing near Nanaimo and the sailors being rescued from seas over twenty feet high with winds gusting sixty-five knots. They'd set out from Vancouver in much more benign conditions, despite a meteorologist advising them the night before that winds on race day might reach sixty knots. Some of the boats registered, of about sixty in the running, pulled out at that point. Not one of them called the Entrance Island lightkeepers to ask for conditions near the finish line of the first leg. Only fifteen boats reached it, including the one on which Seamus was crewing. The race was cancelled at midday, albeit belatedly, but with no loss of lives, very fortunately.

I have now joined the ranks of many lightkeepers who love the meteorological aspect of this work and I would like to keep learning more, in fact. The sky and the sea are so dynamic and ever-evolving, in a state of constant flux. Working out here in Clayoquot Sound is a world away from my Peace River childhood, when we'd stare up at the burnished blue skies with a few insubstantial puffs of cumulus drifting over the northern Rockies and then down at the yellowing, stunted stalks of wheat that had shown such green spring promise. Winter's blizzards and Pine Pass chinooks are the real weather drama queens of the Peace, except for black cumulonimbus clouds bringing hateful midsummer hail, destroyer of dreams. Now I was pleased when I recognized the direction of the offshore wind by observing the height and direction of the waves, or we could tell, while out in our kayaks, exactly how the prevailing current in Templar Channel behind our island behaved during ebb or flood tides. Jeff and I had long-running discussions about the quintessential differences between marine cloud, drifting fog patches and low-level stratus clouds. These topics may not qualify as pillow talk for most people but it gets some of us lightkeepers all excited.

It had been four decades since I studied the weather unit in Geography 101 at UBC but armed with our weather manual, helpful posters of clouds and sea conditions in the radio room and Jeff's admonitions ringing in my ears, I was ready for my first ten-day stint as a relief lightkeeper.

Morning shift. Ugh. I set two alarms for 0400 hours, one beside my bed and the other on the dresser so that I would have to lurch onto my pins and get over there to shut the clanging thing off.

TEN

Staying Warm Haiku

stinging icy breath
infiltrates the rocks, the trees
I'll bake bread today

Lightkeeping
Adventures for the
Formerly Sedentary

WHAT DO YOU *DO* OUT THERE? WE GET ASKED THAT A LOT. NOBODY else really knows what we do around the clock through all four seasons except for other lightkeepers. Certainly no fair-weather visitors or even other Coast Guard workers, whose interactions with us are fairly task-oriented. But I don't doubt that the trained eyes of veteran supervisors and grizzled pilots and long-time work crews take in a few telling details along with the broad strokes when they arrive on a lightstation.

We look after flooding basements, leaking roofs, plugged eavestroughs and everything else in between. We make sure the light in the actual lighthouse is turning and flashing brightly and that condensation, snow, sea spray and wind-borne grime do not prevent it from being seen. We keep the engines running and the furnaces humming and if we can't fix them, we call in a Coast Guard work crew, but only after we've tried every possible way to keep the equipment functioning, often with the good advice of one or more veteran lightkeepers. We shake and check two dozen fire extinguishers and a slew of fire and carbon monoxide alarms every month and we refuel the winch house engine and the domestic tanks of the residences. We mow and clean and paint and sharpen and dig and plant and trim and many other active verbs in order to maintain a safe and shipshape lightstation.

On dry days we haul our household recycling to the large station bins and then transfer the lot into bonnets, which are labelled as to contents and weight. We hoist these bonnets onto the winch line hook and send them down to sea level and a waiting workboat, which takes them back to their Coast

Guard ship. All glass, plastic, metal and assorted returnable containers are recycled. Spent oil, shattered window glass, empty paint cans and the like are contained in special drums called over-packs and shipped off as well. Several times a season, on lovely Friday afternoons especially, we collect the plastic bottles, awful disintegrating hunks of Styrofoam and other flotsam that lands on Lennard's beaches, and we sort, clean and bag that as well.

Jeff sends reports in every month for the BC Coastal Waterbird and Beached Bird Survey, which means walking around the island once a month at low tide to see if there are any dead birds on our rocks and reefs. Jeff photographs these fairly rare occurrences, with the saddest sight being an emaciated snowy owl. Starvation and the ingestion of plastic "confetti" and other man-made junk is the suffering lot of birds like Cassin's auklets. Cape Beale lightkeepers reported a mass die-off of several dozen starving Cassin's auklets in the winter 2014–15 seabird survey. Jeff also photographs and reports significant whale sightings to the Cetacean Society, and several years in early March we've spotted the first of the thousands of grey whales heading north during their annual spring migration. Lightkeepers at all stations report sea mammals in severe distress, especially those wounded by ship's props or caught up in nets or crab traps, or shot by cruel jerks with shotguns, in the hopes that a BC marine rescue team will be able to help the suffering animals.

I was fortunate to begin working on Lennard Island when I started my first shift as a relief keeper. Knowing where certain tools and gear were kept when work crews needed them, being able to pull together many meal options from my own fridge, freezer and pantry instead of sticking to the careful rations I've allotted myself, or us, when working at someone else's station—all these little things add up to a sense of familiarity and ease. Not to mention the comfort of sleeping in our own bed with my preferred pillow and not having to search high and low for kitchen implements and work tools. In my first six months, I worked as an assistant keeper on Lennard five separate times for varying lengths of time, from five days to three weeks, while Jeff went off to work on Trial and Pachena or when Tony Greenall, the principal keeper on Lennard, went out to work at Quatsino and Entrance.

Lightstations with three full-time residents like ours, all qualified, able and willing to work relief, are often asked to work because two of us can hold

Caroline gets ready to work on Lennard in 2008. The glamour never quits!

the fort on the home station while the third person handles the assignment elsewhere. This is especially true for short notice medical and family emergency situations when there is a helicopter or a lifeboat already en route to take one or two of us away. A flurry of packing food, clothing, laptops and books into a couple of large plastic totes ensues. My list-making compulsion and thrifty accumulation of meals in freezer containers comes in handy at times like these.

But Jeff and I did not go through all this effort and change in order to live apart for weeks or even months once we were finally living together. Fortunately no fewer than nine stations of the twenty-seven in BC are run by couples, and they tend to be well-run stations with stable and supportive long-time lightkeepers, people who know how to work together as a team and who don't waste a lot of time and energy on power struggles. Of course, couples also tend to want to go on holidays together so Jeff and I were in demand to fill in for other vacationing pairs. A single keeper would then come in to replace Jeff on Lennard as the assistant keeper while the two of us went off to handle longer assignments at Cape Scott, Quatsino, Nootka, Chrome Island, Pachena Point and Estevan Point, to name six stations run by couples during our first seven years on the lights.

It's still more pleasant to work at home, especially for a gardener like myself, but being able to fly off to places as scenic and historic as Nootka or

Cape Scott together, or to an entirely new station, is also exciting. And half the excitement is getting there by flying over islands and true coastal wilderness, looking down and seeing whales and other more unusual creatures like pale, round sunfish, big sailboats with colourful spinnakers, or tugs towing an entire fishing resort behind them, not to mention flying low enough to see caves and waterfalls—all these amazing sights never, ever become mundane to me. I practically have to pinch myself after a particularly brilliant flight with a cheerful pilot over scenes that tourists and working photographers pay hundreds or thousands of dollars to experience.

Ideally, when we arrive on a new station to work there is time allotted for one or both of the resident keepers to tour us around to all the pertinent sites, like the best sea observation spots, the engine room, the radio room, the sea-sampling site and instruments if applicable, and familiarize us with the winch and high line system or the derrick and rail car system for handling freight and heavy loads from ship to shore.

But sometimes this helpful tour isn't possible because the weather is deteriorating or our arrival has already been delayed by bad weather for a day or more. Sometimes the resident keepers must get out immediately in order make their booked and paid-for holiday flight so the helicopter keeps rotors running while we all work hard to unpack our gear and load the departing keepers' luggage, and then it's a hasty round of hugs and handshakes and within mere minutes the helicopter must depart. We had this situation in reverse while at Cape Scott after one Christmas, with high winds starting to kick up a fuss and a cold rain commencing as well. We all worked together like old hands as the helicopter's rotors roared over our heads, handling a fragile flat-screen television in its cardboard box from one to the other and into the waiting wagon and then getting our totes stashed neatly into the hold. We just made it to the Port Hardy airport in time for Seamus to catch a commercial airplane flight so he could be at his work on time the next morning.

Mindful of this reality, there is usually a flurry of emails or phone calls exchanged before our arrival as to the particulars, explaining temperamental machinery or offering a heads-up regarding a maintenance crew or a ship coming in to deliver something or to fix something vital on their station. At

Estevan Point, we once prepared an old tractor for its final flight, making sure the fuel was drained before pushing it into position as far away from trees or the many guy wires from the telecommunications towers as possible. Then we eased it onto a heavy-duty net and removed its tires to cut down on the weight. Donning our hard hats, we watched as veteran pilot Len Shorkey approached in the Bell 212 dangling a long cable and a hook, skillfully avoiding the obstacle course below until Jeff grabbed the hook and secured it to the net, which now encircled the tractor. Up it went, whizzing through the air until it was gently deposited on the deck of the waiting Coast Guard ship. We watch sling-ops like other grown-ups watch cranes and big machines at city building sites. I feel like cheering, and often do, when the training and finesse of the pilot above and all our prep work below result in a graceful and disaster-free flight.

Then there is the issue of housing while doing relief stints. Sometimes we are invited to move into the principal keeper's home, or the assistant's, or, if available, the spare house, which is also used by work crews. If we need to be housed in someone else's home, there is usually a tour of the kitchen equipment and gadgets, the needs and personalities of pets (we've looked after dogs, cats, fish and a ferret so far with no fatalities), and the personalities and issues of neighbours, if any. Thankfully, no one has asked us to tend any reptiles, which is where I would have to draw the line. Pythons are not proper pets. Priority tasks are listed, like transferring fuel to one of the residences before the domestic tank runs dry or pressure-washing walkways, fuel tanks, eaves or specific buildings in order to keep the ever-present coastal cocktail of salt, mould and airborne grime from creating unsightly or slippery surfaces. In the summer, pressure-washing precedes painting. Some lightkeepers hand their fellow lightkeepers a long list of dirty, smelly jobs they've avoided doing for months (or years), while others are delighted if we do anything more than routine duties, like repainting a tired crew house basement floor or deep-cleaning an engine room. We aim to leave every place where we work as shipshape as we found it or better and we'd much rather do some useful work than twiddle our toes between daytime weather reports.

I've worked alone—i.e., without Jeff but with another lightkeeper—on Lennard, Nootka and Chatham Point lightstations to date. I do get more

Caroline washes the John Deere tractor on Lennard Island.

writing done without his company but it's not as much fun, to be honest. I
don't go on long rambling walks by myself into the wilderness unless I've got
a big and/or smart dog for company. I do not fancy being bear or cougar fare,
so I take short perfunctory "good for me" strolls. I've been asked why we don't
own a gun for protection and I'd always thought, wrongly, that firearms weren't
allowed on lightstations except in special circumstances, like exemptions for
experienced hunters who go out for a moose or elk every fall. And I'd read
about historic conflicts where people were dealing with power struggles or
alcohol or mental health issues. If you are fortunate enough to gaze on the
vertiginous spine of Cape St James, contemplate the assistant running around
the buildings pursued by the principal... armed with a rifle. Amazingly, in well
over a century of lightkeeping in BC, no homicides have been documented.
But if dark thoughts could kill, at least half of us would have been laid low
already. Having looked this rule up, it seems that as long as authorities are
satisfied that a lightkeeper is trained with firearms, they are allowed. If we
lived on a station besieged by starving cougars, especially if we had young

children, I'd consider it very seriously, but we don't. Basically, wildlife isn't nearly as big a threat as the volatility of humans living and working on the same isolated patch of earth.

When working away from Lennard my biggest problem, besides being stuck with the early shift more often than not—a grim fact of life for a night owl like me—was, yet again, being able to be in touch with Jeff. When I worked at Chatham Point, the station satellite dish for the internet wasn't working. The only way to access my email was if I used an air card in the principal's house, which he kindly let me do, but I hated to abuse his hospitality so I used it only twice in eight days. Chatham did have shaky cell phone connection, thanks to a tower across Johnstone Strait on top of Discovery Mountain, but I had to stand out in the inevitably pissing rain across from the engine room, on just the right corner of the fuel shed steps, facing the mountaintop tower and yelling into the phone. Even then half the calls dropped. Sigh. Many lightkeepers have sighed, sworn and sighed some more before me.

I came across a letter echoing my laments in beautiful copperplate handwriting, dated October 24, 1913. It was from lightkeeper Robert Pollock, stationed on Lennard Island, to Captain G. Robertson, Agent in Victoria for Lighthouse Service in the Department of Marine and Fisheries Canada.

> We feel the want of the telephone very much, but I keep up a pressure of air at Station in case anything should happen that I would have to notify the people on shore…. I forgot to mention re. Telephone that Mr. Nicholson examined the instrument and went over the line and with one exception (which he rectified) found it all right. It gave out the night he left here so the trouble is either on the other side or the cable is broken. Hoping we may soon have it working again.
>
> I am
> Yours truly
> Robt Pollock

So the poor man was relying on the station foghorn (hence the remark about keeping up the air pressure, which means attentive and labour-intensive feeding of wood or coal to the boiler) to alert residents in the Chesterman

Beach area should someone on Lennard Island break a leg or suffer appendicitis or begin giving birth prematurely. VHF radios and the ALN system were not invented yet. And of course, we likely all nodded our heads and made rueful clucking noises at the mention of someone else fixing the phone problem only to have it malfunction immediately once he'd left the island. *C'est la bloody vie*, we lightkeepers mutter in bilingual unison. Then I recall the civil servant, who shall remain unnamed, who airily declared that lightkeepers weren't necessary because citizens with cell phones walking on the beaches of British Columbia could call for help if they noticed a boat in trouble. I wish I was making this up. The Coast Guard motto is "Safety First, Service Always." Our steel-toed footwear, ear protectors, hard hats, basic and full-on respirator gear and assorted gloves help us not slip and smash ourselves up when the weather is foul, which it so often is. We've all taken hard tumbles, wrecked our knees and ankles, mashed our thumbs and strained our backs lifting something too heavy, or lifting it the wrong way despite knowing better. We have good first aid kits in every main building as well as eye-wash stands.

Like other veteran lightkeepers, Jeff and I now have our own supply of antibiotics and painkillers on hand, should we ever be forced to wait days for a medevac, with broken limbs, abscessed teeth or other conditions pushing us well past our pain threshold. Once, I had a front crown fall out several weeks before Christmas and there was nothing for it but to carry on for the coming months as the principal keeper was away on extended medical leave. Our wonderful dentist in Victoria couriered all the gear and instructions for taking dental impressions to the Tofino Lifeboat Station, which they promptly delivered to us along with our regular mail. We watched a YouTube demonstration several times as advised. Then we mixed up the goop and Dr. Jeff and I manoeuvred the first of two plates filled with it into my mouth. A Coast Guard helicopter was, most fortuitously, on its way south with a work crew and when we explained our situation, they dropped down and took the box with my dental impressions away, all within one hour of the lifeboat delivering it. My friends in Victoria, bless them, picked it up and took it to the dentist and when the temporary tooth was ready, my friends took it to the base so a helicopter flying north could bring it to me. It fit perfectly!

When I first started relief work, I had the standard occupational first aid course and a remote marine first aid course under my belt. But these certificates expired after three years so I needed to get off the island and out to a place large enough to sponsor the appropriate level of training in order to keep working. I have managed to do it twice during visits to my family in the Okanagan, including a memorable Mother's Day weekend combined with the latest origami techniques in the splinting of limbs and updated cardiac arrest training.

One other fear about being a relief lightkeeper with fairly chronic insomnia is that I'll sleep in and miss a weather report. I've done it. Twice in seven years. It happens to us all and it is humbling and mildly mortifying. Sometimes a good day of work, as a lightkeeper and as a writer, depends on whether I've had a few hours of restless sleep or a blissfully uninterrupted eight hours of being absolutely comatose.

We sign oaths too, for every single work assignment as relief keepers, or else we don't get paid. What the oath (or solemn affirmation) means is basic common sense: that we don't blab or otherwise confide to the media about sensitive and potentially legal situations like search and rescue missions, poaching, vandalism or any VHF radio communication overheard pertaining to such missions—or any other topic, for that matter, as all VHF communication is deemed privileged and private. This doesn't mean we cannot raise any other issues publicly or cannot mightily disagree with federal decisions affecting other aspects of our lives. We are citizens in a democracy after all, even those of us ill-suited to the machinations of bureaucracies. Full-time lightkeepers are represented by union members who can speak freely about our working conditions of course, and retired lightkeepers can and do, bless them, blast away at inanities as they see fit.

In any case, it is not a violation of the oath or the Coast Guard code of values and ethics for me, like any other adult at Careers Day, to tell any schoolchild or individual reader in this country what it is that lightkeepers actually do, or the history of our lighthouses and examples of our assistance in situations where mariners, aviators, hikers and wildlife were in trouble. The public has every right to know we exist and to know what we do to serve them.

Every single lightstation in BC has a well-thought-out rationale for being placed where it is and it's usually to warn mariners of imminent danger. But

Nootka Lightstation is an exception as it signals the entrance to Friendly Cove, a frequent refuge from harsh open sea conditions for boats of all shapes and sizes. It was declared a heritage lighthouse in 2014 and rightfully so as it adds its steady flash—and has since 1911—to one of the most important historic places in the entire province. One friend tells me that if he were the minister of education in BC, he'd arrange for every schoolchild to visit Nootka Island, the place where, for better and for worse in the late 1700s, with the Spanish, British and Americans all battling it out for fur trade supremacy, BC as a territory was born. The First Nations were treated abominably by most of the invaders, as usual, although Native warriors also wreaked bloody havoc on some ship's crews in retaliation. The cruelty of the Spanish toward non-compliant women in particular is still spoken of by Mowachaht elders today.

School visits to Nootka (and I'd add Alert Bay and 'Ksan, near Hazelton) would be a brilliant idea but only the lucky children of Gold River would likely have such an opportunity in this era. As a UBC undergraduate student I majored in sociology but I took all my available elective courses in fine arts history. As well as taking one studio art course with Toni Onley and history courses like Latin American Art and Architecture and Contemporary Art, I studied Primitive Art, which is what they called it back then, with Professor Audrey Hawthorn, a distinguished art historian. Being at Nootka was like going back in time to the darkened basement classroom in the old UBC library, watching Audrey's amazing collection of slides of masks and totem poles. Her passion for the artistry and skill of BC First Nations' master carvers has stayed with me.

I have yet to arrive at Friendly Cove's long public dock on the *Uchuck III*, a converted 1940s minesweeper, but we've admired it and photographed it many times during our relief work there. Watching kayakers being raised or lowered from the deck to the water is a treat to see and one day I would like to actually be in my own kayak being hoisted by the *Uchuck's* crane too. At low tide, Jeff and I have scrambled up the two rocky islets beside San Rafael Island, which the lightstation actually sits atop of, to the cairns for Captains Cook, Quadra and Vancouver. From the wraparound deck of the crew house where we stayed, we could look across Nootka Sound at Bligh Island (yes, the very same *Mutiny on the Bounty* Bligh guy) and admire the trees from afar—Jeff had in fact planted a good many of them in the early 1980s. Another place we, and thousands of others visit annually on Nootka Island proper—again, accessible to us at low tide only—is the former Catholic church. We go there to admire the form, if not the content, of the stained glass windows donated by the government of Spain in 1957, the historic black and white photographs of Yuquot village and the massive 1950s carvings inside what is now the community hall for the Gold River–based Mowachaht-Muchalaht First Nation's summer camp.

Yuquot has been a traditional summer fishing camp for over forty-two hundred years, with Tahsis, sheltered at the head of a long inlet, as the traditional winter residence. But in the 1960s, the Yuquot villagers were lured to Gold River with promises of mill jobs and new housing. Fortunately, for the children and teens in particular, the long tradition of summer camps on their territory provides an opportunity to experience the same elements, the sights and sounds, of this place as their ancestors.

Jeff and I have never worked at Nootka Lightstation during the busy summer season, with the *Uchuck III* coming in with tourists several times a week and hundreds of campers in the meadow or, for that matter, the steady procession of hikers on the Nootka Trail. It's a busy station and the lightkeepers there have traditionally handled many medical emergencies due to the sheer numbers of sports fishers, campers and hikers in the area.

During our first relief stint, and with permission from Ray and Terry Williams, the only permanent residents of Yuquot—they alone did not make the move to Gold River—we were shown a fallen totem pole beside their home. Eleven carvers had created this magnificent pole to present to Viscount Willingdon, a progressive Liberal Englishman with the interesting moniker of Freeman Freeman-Thomas. He was the governor general of Canada from 1926 to 1931 and he came to Yuquot in 1929, the visit a rare honour from such a high-ranking official. He graciously accepted the totem pole and asked for it to stay and stand in the village as a symbol of his friendship. The pole finally fell in 1994 and in the traditional way it is being allowed to rest in place until its cedar body returns to earth itself. I added Viscount Willingdon to my list of interesting and enlightened people to further investigate. Of the master carvers who made this pole, only the anglicized name of their leader,

"Captain Jack," has survived, but it would be interesting research to find out more. Thankfully, this pole stayed put instead of being carted away by scholarly jackals or surreptitiously sold off to the highest bidder like the Yuquot Whalers' Shrine in 1904, which is still in the basement of a museum in New York City.

At the west-facing edge of the ancient fishing camp meadow stands a monumental carving of a welcome figure looking out to sea, made by Yuquot-born master carver Sanford Williams and two apprentices. Our walks nearly always took us past a cedar grieving figure in the first cemetery, another powerful work by Sanford, whose studio is at the water's edge of Friendly Cove. Now on the Nootka Trail, we'd walk past several cemeteries and their graves, some with carved granite headstones, one with an old sewing machine beside it, one with a recently made bentwood box holding the bones in the traditional way. Beautiful sombre cemeteries overrun by salal in some spots where relatives no longer tend the graves, graced with daffodils in spring...

As with the ancient Haida village of Skun'gwaii, there is a palpable sense of history even in the deserted winter meadow that was once a bustling village of hundreds of people living in longhouses facing the water. This atmosphere

Caroline and Molly Brown follow the fence line put up by Danish settlers near Cape Scott Lightstation.

is enhanced by the music of the surf riffling through thousands of polished stones, all clinking together on the immense curving beaches, and the abundance of all kinds of vocal birds and howling wolves and exhaling whales in the cove feasting on herring spawn. The word that comes to mind is overused but that's because it's true: awesome.

This job gives me the unparalleled opportunity to live in magical places like Nootka, where I've worked at least seven times now, for as long as ten weeks at a stretch. It's taken me to tiny Chrome Island, where there are petroglyphs carved into the granite rock face that depict a Spanish captain wearing his distinctive metal helmet alongside a Salish chief in his elaborate headdress. Other carvings portray fish and deer and female fertility. This work, physical and mundane as it is, gave me the chance to stumble by accident upon the fenced grave of Nels Jensen, the founder of Cape Scott's pioneering Danish colony, which lasted, despite heartbreaking natural and political disasters, from 1897 to 1907. A tiny Danish flag is placed beside his cross. The hayfields for their gentle dairy cattle have returned to wild meadows and given way to sand dunes deeply furrowed by stormy seas, and only the wind-polished stubs of fence posts are still standing. It's grim history. But it's glorious fodder for any writer's imagination.

I've begun work on a children's story about ghostly games in the fog...

ELEVEN

Hummingbird War Dodoitsu #2

Four gram warriors zooming
Angry whirring winds resound
How many men do you know
Fight over flowers?

Mishaps in Manual Labour

DউRING MY FIRST WEEK OF WORKING THE EARLY SHIFT, IT WAS HOT. I mean the actual heat of a round yellow August sun blasted through the fog of Fogust in Tofino. One day I donned a pair of Jeff's ancient shorts and a tank top (in order to better tan my flabby muscles) and set out to master the Mighty Gas Lawn Mower. Lennard Island Lightstation has an abundance of lumpy lawns that can only be trimmed with push mowers and weed whackers. The only nice flat lawn is the helipad and it is the only one that can be mowed with the little John Deere mower-tractor, a sweet task indeed as absolutely no muscle power is required.

During the eight years we had the Motherlode Bookstore up and running, we had a massive lawn and used an old electric mower at first, which was tiny and in no way up to the task of mowing a lawn so large. Then we bought a virtuous non-polluting reel mower, meaning all push, no gas or electricity. That gave us a very good workout indeed. But here on Lennard Island, the side hills, sheer acreage and bumpy, boggy terrain, plus the hauling and heaving of heavy gas mowers from one level to the next, is a real test of muscle power.

On that sunny, warm day when I first pushed the Gas Beast as a rookie relief keeper, I half-listened as I got the verbal instructions. Surely all I needed to know was how to start it, and if it wasn't doing a good job, to stop it and clean the underside if it was clogged with wet grass. With that straight, I set out to just push it around and around for several hours. But going up a slope, I tried to turn the Beast and quickly realized I didn't know how to stop or even slow down the machine. Furthermore, I had it revved up so high that I couldn't run behind it and read the instructions on the handles, or wherever they were hidden, at the same time.

I was rattled and the Beast had pushed me back down the slope, thanks to gravity, and I found myself backed into a big thorn-filled blackberry bush. The mower was steadily shoving me backward and I was going to end up impaled on a thousand thorns if I didn't opt for a shorter-lived bout of pain by squeezing out sideways and getting myself back in front of the Beast. I did this, incurring the expected flesh wounds, but I also managed to shut the thing off so I could decipher the instructions. Which I ought to have done more thoroughly in the first place, of course, as it was the first time I'd ever used a gas mower in my life. Duh!

At Chatham Point Lightstation on a hot summer day, during another relief stint, I was pushing the station lawn mower across a steep side hill for the first time. I was thinking about how many a poor farmer who'd put slow but sure-footed workhorses out to pasture in order to modernize with a new tractor had met an untimely end, rolling under the mechanized marvel as it overbalanced on the slope. I remembered my dad, who had made just such a transition on our homestead, stating these words like a mantra: *Never plow across the slope. Always up or down the hill.*

I believe I've mentioned my intense dislike, call it a phobia if you will, of snakes. When I was a small girl, I stepped into a writhing mass of baby garter snakes in a slough and could not get my panicky little feet out of them fast enough. Truly, this was the stuff of lifelong nightmares. Chatham Point is sunny and has wonderful gardens and a fruit orchard that serves as a tasty smorgasbord for all kinds of wildlife, especially hungry deer and bears. It also welcomes garter snakes, like the little green and black striped one that right then slithered under my lawn mower.

I shrieked a Very Bad Word and somehow overbalanced on the slope and like Jack and Jill, the wretched mower, the snake and I all tumbled down the bloody hill, landing, of course, right in a big blackberry hedge. I sprang to my feet, cussed sundry articles some more and hauled the infernal machine back up the slope again. The principal lightkeeper's wife, a lovely and devout Christian woman, came running down the path to see if I was okay. I assured her that only my dignity was damaged and I apologized for swearing so much.

(I should just hang a laminated sign in permanent laundry marker around my neck to that effect.) She claimed not to have heard a word but she did smile constantly and in a most understanding sort of way...

At Estevan Point Lightstation, I encountered the largest expanse of lightstation lawn yet, with many roots, rocks and lumpy bits to deal with. Also, snakes, big, well-nourished garter snakes and small lively fellas, lots and lots of snaky variety. The good news was that the John Deere mower-tractor could handle 98% of the terrain so I hopped on it and three to four hours later, after at least a dozen stops to empty the bulging grass bags onto designated piles (wary as ever of snakes springing up in the bags, a fear that never once materialized), my mission was completed. The worst thing that ever happened was when I drove past a blackberry patch one day and saw a snake *dangling at eye level!* WTF! What was the creature doing up on a thorny blackberry bush nearly two metres off the ground? Going after lovely, ripe blackberries I surmised, but rational thoughts came later. An erratic zigzag spoiled the look of the aesthetically soothing patterns I was mowing onto the lawn that particular day.

Tractor mowing did provide something akin to a gym workout, as my arms were constantly battling the steering wheel and my core abdominal muscles were tensing and tightening as I leaned and lurched on the tractor seat. By the end of my first full year of relief keeping, I'd lost more than four kilos of excess weight, and by the next year, the same again. We created a gym in the former engine room at Lennard Island and over several years we resident keepers have added a treadmill, an elliptical machine, a rowing machine, assorted free weights, a yoga mat, a rubber ball and my mountain bike mounted on a heavy-duty trainer. We moved in a TV and CD player and watched home improvement and travel shows while we huffed and puffed our way into much better shape than during our book-peddling years. By the end of my sixth year as a lightkeeper, I'd lost a total of eleven kilos, which is just fine as long as I can keep them off permanently and keep building strong core, arm and leg muscles as well. I am well on my way to one of my ten goals for living on the lights, along with reclaiming a flexible and sturdy back, which, as fellow dodgy back sufferers will appreciate, now only goes out once a year, if that. Compared to crawling around in agony at least four to six times a year during the previous high-stress decades, I feel almost invincible. But don't ask me to extol my fit and healthy progress in fluent Spanish while accompanying myself on a cello just yet.

Some stations we've worked, like Nootka, Cape Scott, Pachena and Estevan Point, offer long stretches of hiking trails lightkeepers can use to get some exercise during the three hours between weather reports. Most lightkeepers view Saturdays and Sundays as days to enjoy more of our own recreation and hobbies between weather reports since we are less likely to expect a helicopter or a ship. Work comes first, of course, if we do have a ship coming in to pick up or deliver freight or a helicopter landing for any reason.

One lovely spring Saturday at Nootka Lightstation, Jeff and I headed out for a walk, intending to go as far as Third Beach, a good hour of steady walking. Then the plan was to turn back and walk home again at a more leisurely pace, allowing us time to take photographs and use the binoculars to watch for birds and for any sight of a local trio of grey whales spouting. Besides our hand-held VHF radio, cameras and binoculars, we had with us

Caroline brings fuel up to fill the domestic tanks while Heidi looks longingly at her KONG under the tractor.

the usual accoutrements for hiking the Nootka Trail: bear spray, bear bangers (noisemakers replicating gunshots), a piercing whistle I wore around my neck for easy access, an air horn, which is a can of compressed air that emits an awful blast of noise, and two gleaming Sitka spruce hiking sticks with pointy brass ends, handmade by Seamus for us one Christmas.

We also had a plan we'd discussed beforehand should a bear, cougar or wolf pack show up for the hike. I would get Molly Brown, our border collie–cross, on her leash, if she wasn't already, while Jeff would pick up little Lucy, a Bichon Frise that belonged to Mark and Joanne Tiglmann, the resident lightkeepers away on vacation. Jeff would tuck Lucy under one arm like a football. Then we would use our noisemakers and our hiking sticks to defend the four of us against all comers, side by side or back to back if we were encircled by a pack. Oh, and we'd also use our VHF radios to yell for help on channels 6 and 66, the local working channels in Nootka Sound, after a mayday on channel 16, in the hopes that our neighbour in Yuquot, Ray Williams, or one of his sons or grandsons, would hear us and come roaring down the Nootka Trail on his ATV, armed to the teeth.

The Williams family had lost four dogs over the decades to the wolf pack that ranged between Yuquot and places unknown on Nootka Island. We'd met one of the dogs during a previous relief stint, a shy, sweet and long-legged young animal, but poor Iggy was no match for a hungry pack of wolves. We'd heard of another big dog who'd disappeared without a trace as it followed its owner on a walk between Yuquot and Jewitt Lake, a well-treed one-kilometre walk we took almost daily with the dogs. So we kept our pair of hounds leashed at all times unless we were walking along the long beaches and even then, we made sure they came promptly when called and didn't run away too far from us or venture up near the tree line.

We had both dogs unleashed as we climbed over a pile of jumbled drift-wood as high as a house separating two long beaches. It was a natural corner between Second and Third Beach, with several two-storey boulders holding back the sea on one side and a cliff forming a solid barricade on the land side and all the driftwood logs jammed between them. Jeff had to pick Lucy up—the logs were tossed up like massive matchsticks, jammed between two immovable forces, and it was simply too much for her wee legs. Molly is a little mountain goat so she was able to scramble up, around or over the logs, treating them like nature's own agility course.

"Is that a wolf?" asked Jeff.

I looked up from the huge red cedar log I was hoisting myself over and saw what looked like a long-legged German shepherd staring down at us from about five metres away. I blinked hard and stared.

"Yes!" I finally blurted, then I yelled, feeling my vocal cords tighten with fear, "No! Molly! No! Come here now!"

Brave little Molly charged at the wolf, which was so surprised that he bolted off. Molly figured out that the note of terror in my voice was no bluff and scooted back to me, and I leashed her up. Lucy was already in the football position under Jeff's arm. We stood still and watched as the wolf loped away on his impossibly long springy legs, casually bounding to the higher, tree-lined side of Third Beach, where he stopped and looked back at us.

Later I would describe his look as much like Clint Eastwood gazing into the middle distance at lesser hombres: scornful, suspicious and a little annoyed as he inspected the two edible dogs. But also, very clearly, he was unafraid of us. Add a well-chewed cheroot, a poncho and a battered cowboy hat and you'd have the right impression of this alpha male wolf.

"Get outa here!" I managed to croak, in an obviously fearful voice. Jeff managed to holler at him to get lost, which struck us as hilarious later on, given where the wolf had spent his entire life. We forgot about our noise-making equipment entirely. We hustled ourselves and our leashed dogs back home on the beaches all the way, even though it was like walking on slopes made of ball bearings, which my knees did not appreciate. But we did not trust the heavily wooded Nootka Trail, in case the wolf decided to be proactive and stalk us, waiting for just the right moment to pounce on one of the dogs, leash or no leash. We didn't know how hungry he was or if the pack, led by the alpha female, was also in the 'hood.

The only other time I'd encountered a wolf before was at Cape Scott Lightstation after delivering the last weather report of my shift. Again, I had Molly with me, and as we came out of the radio room building, I fumbled with my flashlight and the doorknob to close the door against the extreme winds and heavy rain underway. Molly barked her high-alarm bark and rushed at a skinny grey dog-shape illuminated by the outdoor light triggered by movement over at the spare house. Molly charged at the wolf, ripping the loosely held leash out of my left hand. The scraggly, undersized wolf disappeared into the dark toward the helipad, but once again Molly Brown came back to me quickly, having done her protective duty and displayed righteous umbrage.

I yelled Jeff's name twice and stared through the pelting rain and inky darkness at the house with the porch light on, the house where Jeff was asleep—and rightly so, as he had to start work in less than five hours. The noise of the storm drowned out my voice. The rain smeared my glasses and I could not see well through the wretched things at all. A loose chunk of metal was banging above me on the workshop roof, a casualty of the wild December weather.

I knew we had to wait for daylight and for the weather to calm down but I really wanted to get that lethal piece of metal detached from the roof before the winds snatched it away. A flying chunk of metal roofing like that could decapitate a person or a dog. Morbid thoughts notwithstanding, there was nothing for it but to get myself and my dog to safety at the house or else hole up in the radio room all night. I didn't have the hiking stick at that time, which I now call my "wolf whacker" or "cougar poker." I grabbed the air horn can from the radio room—the keepers at Cape Scott have had black bears ambling between their house and the radio room before, and Todd and Harvey had warned us when we arrived that the wolf pack was howling nearby—and then Molly and I walked to the house, with me walking backward half the way, my flashlight swinging from side to side and between the buildings to catch any glint of wolfish eyeballs.

I am here, typing away in a warm room, so the Astute Reader knows I made it safely and lost neither my life nor my dog's to that ravenous wolf or her pack that night. In fact, B movies and atavistic folk tales to the contrary, wolves usually attack dogs and other prey before people. They are curious and have been known to stalk human beings but some wildlife biologists claim there is no documented evidence of any *healthy* wolf (emphasis mine) attacking a person anywhere in North America, and that the real culprits are unpredictable wolf-dog hybrids, which have a long-documented history of attacks on humans, especially children. Coastal wolves have a varied diet with diverse items on the menu including spawning salmon, barnacles, herring roe, chitons and dead seals. But when wolves live near wilderness parks and hiking trails, they can lose their fear of people if they are fed by ignorant humans, and the result of this meddling has led to campers being bitten and, sadly, wolves being shot.

Our dog is our brave and vocal bodyguard, and she is our early warning protection system while we work and when we head out for walks. Molly Brown has run bears up trees at Estevan Point Lightstation and once warned me, from inside the house, that a greedy big black bear was investigating the strawberry patch. She heard the sound of the rocks being flipped from the protective netting over the berries, there ostensibly to protect them from birds. But what bear could resist ripe strawberries as a break from the ocean's wrack line smorgasbord of half-dead hermit crabs and rotting salmon carcasses? A few good blasts of the air horn sent him crashing off through the salal and back to the wrack line that day.

We lightkeepers always have ear protectors on while mowing lawns and using the pressure washer, so it's good to know you have a dog to watch your back. While focused on these tasks, we are virtually deaf to the outside world, and we spend a lot of time bent over in what cougars see as the prey position. I'm apparently too concerned about harmless garter snakes to look way up in fear of a cougar eyeing me from an overhanging tree branch. I like to think that the noise of the motor is enough to deter a wild animal but I know they spend a lot of time watching us and I would never underestimate their intelligence on that score. We don't even know cougars are around most of the time, unless we come across their tracks.

Human beings are another kind of adventure, though. Molly is downright embarrassing when pilots and work crews visit the station. She leaps up and attempts to lick all newcomers despite our yells of "Down, Molly, down!" She loses her mind and forgets her manners when new people arrive, friendly to a fault. She also forgot who it was she belonged to when we were doing a six-week relief stretch at Estevan Point one summer.

When hikers arrive there, they usually stop at the station for a break unless they are behind schedule and high tide is threatening to cover the boulder-strewn beaches they must cross to get to the next campsite on the

Hesquiaht Trail. The lightkeepers have built a fire pit and provide rustic benches and chairs for weary hikers, and there is a flush toilet attached to a nearby workshop, a rare commodity (pardon the near-pun) on any wilderness hiking trail in BC. Hikers can refill their canteens with filtered water as well, and sign the guest book. Having hikers sign in at lightstations can give us crucial information if things go wrong on the wilderness trails or if there are urgent family emergencies and those hikers need to be alerted. Lightkeepers can play a vital role in locate-and-evacuate missions.

The first time it happened, we had our hands full and our ear protectors on while I mowed the lawns and Jeff pressure-washed the assistant's house. We each thought Molly was hanging out with the other. When we stopped working for the day, we finally realized she was not inside or outside... We called and called but no furry black pup bolted out of a building or out of the bush either. The latest set of hikers had been gone for hours by then, but she hadn't followed them when they'd set out.

I thought she'd been taken by a cougar or a bear while we worked at our noisy tasks. Maybe a lone wolf or the pack had slunk in and grabbed her since they were rumoured to roam within a few kilometres of the station. We'd been told the pack denned up near Homais, the traditional summer fishing village of the Hesquiaht people a bit north of us, but we weren't sure. I was heartsick as I walked the perimeter of the grounds looking for tracks, for trampled drag marks through the long grass. I walked with my heart actually hurting in my chest and my mind in a state of self-imposed numbness.

Jeff hotfooted down to the beach with our binoculars while I went up the stairs of the ninety-four-metre tower, the tallest lighthouse on the BC coast, to look as far north and south as I could along the bear-infested beaches. Eventually Jeff saw the six hikers arrive on Matlahaw Beach, the first camp-site to the south, seven kilometres away. A tiny black dot on four legs moved among them. We were simultaneously relieved and exasperated.

It was midsummer and it wouldn't be dark until nine o'clock. The tide was out, favouring us. Jeff had only gumboots and old running shoes to choose between so he wore the runners and took off with an air horn, a radio and one of Seamus's hiking sticks, as well as Molly's leash. He had to cross a favourite stretch of food source for bears, the wrack line left by the outgoing tide. When bears are hungry, however, they have their minds occupied solely by the food in front of them. Jeff gave a mother and yearling cub and another single bear a wide berth on his way down to the campsite, much of it horrible hiking on slippery round boulders, the perfect terrain for a sprained ankle. The Billion Boulder Beach nickname for this part of the Hesquiaht Trail is no exaggeration. When he finally got to Matlahaw, one kind hiker gave Jeff her chocolate bar, no doubt noticing his battered running shoes, sweating body and seething but silent distress.

Darkness began to descend. I went back up the tower and from that height I could see a black dot and a tiny human on the final straight stretch of beach with the tide coming in fast. There was a bear in between them and the turnoff to the old boardwalk road that once connected the lightstation to the village of Hesquiaht. I put on my headlamp, grabbed another air horn, my radio and my hiking stick, and headed for the beach, looking up a lot to make sure there wasn't a cougar in the trees. I'd been feeling watched for a while—it was "just a feeling," but I always pay attention to those feelings.

A view of the Estevan Point light tower from the Billion Boulder Beach.

I made it to the end of the boardwalk and out to the beach, where I climbed up onto the biggest rock I could find. I could see the bear still feeding, nose down into the seaweed and dead crabs and whatever else was in the wrack line. So there I was on a big beach boulder waving my headlamp and tooting the air horn to both warn and welcome the weary stragglers. I could see Jeff and Molly giving the bear a lot of space and was relieved that the bear never once looked up from his seafood smorgasbord. Apparently Molly had caught up to the group near the end of the boardwalk, only four hundred metres from the station, but no one wanted to stop and bring the eight-month-old pup back to us, which would have been a mere twenty-minute delay. Grrrr. We did get a very sincere letter of apology from the group later that summer.

The next time it happened, later during that same summer, Molly followed a young couple who hadn't stopped in at the station, slipping right by us. This time I was way up in the tower painting the cupola floor and Jeff was blasting more coastal cocktail grime off the back wall of the spare house. Molly was bored with hanging out at the bottom of the tower (she didn't trust the spiral metal staircase up to where I was working) and she was not fond of the non-stop noise of the pressure washer.

This time, the tide and the oncoming darkness did not favour us but we were able to see a tent at Matlahaw Beach and again, a little black dot on four furry legs. Damn dog!

Next morning at daybreak, Jeff started the long trudge through the slippery rocks in his woefully inadequate footwear. I did his weather reports and watered all the gardens and waited. Seven hours later, the pair of them got back to the station. Molly Brown was very hungry indeed and so was Jeff, even though he'd taken more water and a proper lunch with him, learning after the last episode that he'd really need it. A feeding bear delayed this second expedition by a few more crucial minutes.

Thankfully, 99.5% of the hikers, sailors and kayakers we meet are not as clueless as this oblivious pair, who kept hiking and ignored Jeff's air horn and whistling and yells. They were so lucky I wasn't there with my wolf whacker to embellish a few choice words with them! Then there was the over-aged dude who was reluctant to sign the guest register and who threatened to go up the tower, which we'd already told him was off limits. My radar waggled at the display of attitude, which embarrassed his teenage son greatly. As one anonymous sage explained: *When you are dead, you don't know you are dead. It is difficult only for the others. It is the same when you are stupid.*

But by far the majority of the outdoorsy people we meet are thrilled to be out in this truly wild world, appreciative of clean water for their Thermoses and any fresh-baked cookies, garden tomatoes and cucumbers we've given them to perk up their dried food rations. For us, it's also a chance to shoot the breeze with some amazing and interesting people, all of which adds up to a very good day as an unofficial host in the wilderness.

Caroline, on the walk outside the Estevan Point light's cupola, checks the sunlight recorder, an ingenious "old" technology that magnifies even the most feeble ray of sun through a glass ball and scorches the graph paper at the exact time of the happy event! Lightkeepers then send out each day's data via computer.

I much prefer isolated lightstations, though, to those visited by several hundred or several thousand hikers and kayakers every summer, because if I'm not doing lightkeeper work, I'm writing or I'm thinking about writing.

I embody the attitude of Greta Garbo, albeit a great deal less glamorously than she did, in my John Deere ball cap and steel-toed gumboots. And grubby work clothes in between, of course.

TWELVE

For Certain Bureaucrats in Boats: Choka #1

If your rudders jam
and your radios drop, plop,
& your GPS
marinates in salty air
then fizzles, defunct.

No worries, though, a lighthouse looms!

Your maydays echo
in empty rooms; no one hears.
The light turns, oblivious.

Christmas on
Entrance Island

EXACTLY ONE YEAR AND TWO WEEKS AFTER I'D LEFT MY PUBLISHING job and joined Jeff on Lennard Island, the highest-ranking bureaucrat in Ottawa in charge of the Coast Guard announced that nine BC lightstations would be de-staffed, four of them within two months. That dire news identified Entrance Island, Trial Island, Cape Mudge and Dryad Point lightstations as the first four on the federal chopping block. The next five to be de-staffed within one year were Green Island, Addenbroke Island, Chrome Island, Pachena Point and Carmanah Point.

But the two-month deadline passed by while the lightkeepers' union representatives and our many allies prepared for a war of words. Jeff and I were scheduled to spend our second Christmas on the lights at Entrance Island and we'd put in a request for helicopter transportation for Seamus to join us as well. I must state here that our own BC Coast Guard bureaucrats move mountains in order to reunite lighthouse families at Christmas, and they are incredibly fast when it comes to getting us evacuated for family or medical emergencies.

For days it seemed we'd been packing gear: warm mitts, work gloves, gumboots, two or three climates' worth of hats, *de rigueur* raingear and carefully selected layers of warmth, from long underwear to one semi-snazzy yet not too bulky outfit suitable for Christmas dinner. I live to make lists, as I've said, for the tidy illusion of control and for the simple joy of crossing out completed items with a bright highlighter pen. For this compulsive habit we were both grateful when the Coast Guard 212 helicopter radioed us a two-minute warning—about two hours earlier than we expected.

Jeff, the perennial early bird, had already loaded the station's wagon with boxes of presents and our totes packed with neatly labelled Ziploc bags, the latter filled with pancake dry mix, four kinds of rice, better than usual granola and other more mundane grains. All the non-perishable ingredients—the cans of coconut milk and refried beans, jars of spices, canola and olive oil and homemade gyoza dip, enough food for every day of the twelve days of Christmas we would spend on Entrance Island—were also packed and ready to go, with the little John Deere tractor towing the wagon poised for action, pointed in the direction of the helipad.

Still, my heart went into a little frisson of palpitations when the chopper arrived so early. *Zut alors!* We flew into high gear, stuffing our freezer and fridge items into coolers and heavy-duty plastic totes. For two weeks I'd been baking—sourdough and French bread, tourtière, gyoza, six kinds of cookies, fudge—and prepping dry mixes of biscuit dough and pizza dough and putting it all into the freezer. Jeff had made his trademark nuts and bolts and chocolate cherry flips, and branched out with a very successful innovation, dried cranberry and chocolate chip meringue cookies. He is handy as well as handsome, and he cooks and does dishes too! Form a line, ladies, but I intend to live to ninety-three and we plan to expire together, holding hands, preferably after a mid-afternoon bout of hot sex. But I digress.

The turkey, a hefty thing pushing eight kilos, was flying solo, shoved into the hold of the helicopter by itself, frozen solid and encased in its durable plastic cover. We reasoned we'd be in the air over Vancouver Island for less than an hour and it was December 22. Point being, the noble bird needed to begin defrosting anyway.

More problematic was Molly Brown, recently adopted and only eleven weeks old. She was only somewhat house-trained at this point, as well as a novice to helicopter travel. But Jeff had ordered Mutt Muffs for her, earmuffs specially designed by a pilot who took his pooch along on flights, and Jeff had also built her a sturdy wood and plastic mesh crate. I'd sewn her a plush fleece pillow, which had an old flannelette sheet "envelope" of cedar shavings inside to ward off fleas. Thus equipped, Molly, our Port Alberni SPCA Special, was all set for her first helicopter ride.

I wouldn't be able to give our floors a final mopping or fret about any unwashed breakfast dishes. I was just relieved that our relief keeper would be staying in the crew house so I wouldn't have to worry about leaving a messy home for him. We had to fly across Vancouver Island while the weather held so that the lightkeepers on Entrance Island could leave, one for holidays and the other for another relief assignment. I counted my blessings for having hopped into an early morning shower before commencing the final packing up.

Then I beheld my own Christmas gift, arriving early, in the form of Seamus, jogging up the sidewalk with an ecstatic Molly Brown bouncing along beside him. The pilot had rerouted the itinerary to deliver two other lighthouse family members to stations en route and brought Seamus along for the ride instead of delivering him to Entrance Island on a separate trip. We hadn't seen him since late October and between Molly leaping and all of us laughing and talking at once while madly stuffing perishable foods and fragile presents into the final tote to load the helicopter, it was an emotional flurry!

Jeff and I kept in close touch with Seamus by email at least, and after Jeff diligently worked on several systems to boost our cell phone reception, we were able to stay in touch that way too. Seamus was still working as a sailboat rigger in Sidney and elsewhere on the island using the company van, and earning his international marine trades apprenticeship certificate, a four-year program offered through night school. He wanted to learn how to make sails next. Needless to say, he was racing as a crew member on different sailboats nearly every weekend as well. He was happy, so we were happy.

It was a stellar blue and white and gold West Coast winter day. After a round of hasty hugs to the keepers we were leaving behind on Lennard, we hopped aboard the Bell 212 and lifted off. With our pup wearing her ear protectors in the travel crate alongside us, and all of us wearing our own version of them, we soared above the Beaufort Range, the rocky spine of Vancouver Island. We hadn't experienced a sunny day like this one for weeks it seemed and here we were, with a veteran pilot at the controls and a grizzled engineer in the co-pilot's seat wearing his trademark helmet, labelled

Molly Brown at eight weeks old in her newly made kennel, wearing her ear protectors for helicopter rides.

"SSDD=Same Shit Different Day." I stared down at the mountains and inlets, grinning non-stop, while Jeff shot photos with his long lens the whole way.

Out beyond the sprawling coastal city of Nanaimo and the sprinkling of islands offshore, Newcastle, Protection, Gabriola and Snake, we saw the familiar red and white buildings on a barren green rock. Entrance Island Lightstation, first built in 1875, guards the entrance to Nanaimo Harbour and a cluster of moorages for boats of all sizes, yet it is far enough out in the Salish Sea to serve as a navigational sentinel. The historic lightstation is vital as well to busy seaplanes coming in from Vancouver because the lightkeepers handle a steady stream of requests for updated wind speed and visibility conditions in the harbour. With notoriously shifty fog conditions, the safety of pilots and passengers makes it critical to have trained eyes and radio communication on scene, not a mute and salt-begrimed video camera.

Jason Beukens, a wildlife biologist and the principal lightkeeper on Entrance Island at the time, left us detailed instructions for collecting sea water samples, a new task for me but not for Jeff, as well as a very good bottle of Shiraz, a box of chocolates and a basket of seasonal nuts to crack. We lightkeepers greatly appreciate such hospitable gestures! I was touched that a young bachelor would have a live Christmas tree, which we quickly elevated to a side table due to Molly Brown's curiosity about the dangling candy canes. Jason also had the only living spruce tree on the island cheerily bedecked with strings of lights and a cleverly constructed silver and gold star on top. I was sure ferry passengers and all manner of boaters enjoyed his seasonal tribute. It certainly brightened my spirits to see those dancing lights in the stiff winds and downpours of rain we experienced over the next two weeks.

In spite of the extra work involved in preparing and packing up food supplies and all the rest of our gear in order to live and work away from our home lightstation, I loved doing relief work. Not only did I earn money while I worked as an assistant keeper but Jeff was the acting principal keeper, thereby earning a bit more than he would as the assistant lightkeeper on Lennard Island. The well-worn clichés of taking a busman's holiday and variety being the spice of life definitely hold true for relief lightkeeping as well.

But as one O.W.L. remarked: Relief keeping is wonderful until it isn't. We have hit that wall several times and longed for the familiarity of our home island and our tasty garden veggies, our actual bed and especially our pillows, my writing room and all our reference books. Not to mention the absence of major predators to worry about for ourselves and our dog.

On Entrance, though, I enjoyed seeing the great increase in ocean-going traffic compared to what we saw from Lennard Island; the gleaming white BC Ferries regularly sailed past at twenty knots to and from Duke Point on the island and Tsawwassen on the mainland. Public and private truck ferries hauling containers of produce and other goods to and from the Island. Tugboats lugging barges and log booms non-stop, while intrepid fishers and sailors headed out in all but the stormiest of conditions. Overhead, the seaplanes and commuter planes buzzed us and waggled their wings in response to our waves.

Then there was the new wildlife to check out, as every lightstation has its resident population of critters and birds. On Entrance in December, the notorious overpopulation of garter snakes was safely denned underground. I sincerely hoped not to be asked to work there during the spring or summer when, according to Jeff, who'd spent three weeks there in May, the island practically writhes with the reptiles, which have nowhere else to go.

But Entrance was also home to colonies of sea lions, so much so that tour boats ventured out in the summer months to show the tourists the spectacle of as many as six hundred of the marine giants hauled up onto the sandstone rocks. The noise of their barking during the mating season simply has to be sublimated to white noise by the keepers or else they'd go barking mad themselves. This December, though, there were only nine California sea lions, which I like to think of as the ones with cute upturned noses and long, trailing whiskers, like older English gentlemen in cartoons, harrumphing and grunting, as well as several tawny-gold Steller sea lions. They co-existed quite amicably, floating around with their fins and flippers idly stirring the air like rudders, their black or tawny heads resting on each other's massive bodies with the splendid indolence of Rubens's nudes. There were twenty or thirty harbour seals who also hauled their rotund silvery-black selves up onto the rocks. The two groups of sea mammals kept a respectful distance from each other.

Molly Brown was intrigued by the two river otters that lived under the greenhouse and slipped in and out of several crannies amongst the boulders but fortunately their odorous fishy droppings were of no interest to her. Our old dog, Ben Brown, would have gleefully rolled in their smelly turds and any rotting fish heads they left behind, one of his less desirable traits. We also kept Molly away from them because river otters do kill dogs, especially small pups with no street savvy who blunder along being curious about other species, oblivious to their own mortal danger.

The winter population of birds included oystercatchers, the usual assortment of gulls, two adult eagles and one juvenile eagle. We watched little Molly carefully when the eagles were patrolling their island and I always carried some good throwing rocks in my rain jacket pocket, just in case, but nothing untoward ever occurred. We also watched the shorebirds: flurries of western sandpipers, least sandpipers, semipalmated sandpipers and black turnstones. On the water, we saw Pacific loons, buffleheads, cormorants, common mergansers, surf scoters and our favourites, the harlequin ducks in their winter finery.

Jeff paced the sidewalk between the two houses and added some extra steps to the engine room, declaring that four round trips added up to a mile and so Seamus, Jeff and I, singly, together, with or without Molly Brown, managed to get some daily physical exercise. But it was a valiant fight for fitness, ultimately, up against our high-calorie Christmas fare: a lovely round of brie and six other good cheeses, a heavy, delicious banana-date breakfast cake, the Manitoba chokecherry jam made by Jeff's sister, Lory, and saved for the holidays to complement cream cheese on my homemade bread… well, we were losing the battle of the bulge but we still enjoyed the fresh sea air on our walks, playing the Farming Game and Rummikub, and putting together yet another nautical puzzle. As another lightkeeper remarked, everyone goes out of their way to find lighthouse kitsch and memorabilia for you, so we may as well revel in it. And we all enjoyed cheering on Molly B. as she raced across the cement helipad and launched herself at the densely matted ivy around it as if it were a trampoline grown especially for her recreational use.

I loved standing on the edge of the low-lying island banks when the tide was high and the ocean was rippled and glassy. I'd gaze out over the water when the visibility was so clear I could easily see the lights and buildings of Sechelt, Vancouver and nearby Nanaimo, as well as the Coast Mountains near Whistler, and Mount Baker and the Olympic Peninsula in the state of Washington to the southeast, all of us connected by the immense span of the Salish Sea. On Gabriola Island, so near and yet so far away, were the warm and inviting lights from quintessential West Coast homes tucked in amongst arbutus trees. On still, clear nights, I could even see the lights flash from Ballenas Island Light (de-staffed in the 1990s) and Merry Island Light near Sechelt. I could see several aircraft at different heights circling the amber nighttime glow that I knew was Vancouver International Airport and I would watch the fixed single lights of the commuter seaplanes coming straight toward us, each airborne Cyclops bound for Nanaimo Harbour.

I had my gumboots filled with chilly salt water not once but twice during high tide dips for a sea water sample off the dock, a somewhat precarious operation involving an old-style milk bottle secured to a long pole. I was paying so much attention to getting a water sample from a consistent depth that I neglected to watch for waves, most often the wake from large boats or the ferries. Lesson #1, which also applies to hockey, always keep your head up. Also, never turn your back on the sea, which is also easier said than done. We measured the temperature of the sea water once daily, in two different containers, and used an instrument called a hydrograph to measure the salinity of the water. I've now collected sea samples at three different stations and each one has slightly different equipment, including a completely computerized, hand-held gizmo to measure salinity and temperature at Quatsino.

As usual, Jeff worked the morning shift and I worked the afternoon shift for our weather reports, collected by Victoria Coast Guard's MCTS crew. We were joined on the ALN radio circuit by Chrome Island, Merry Island and Trial Island. The main sea-state difference at Entrance Island, on the east coast of Vancouver Island, compared to Lennard, is that there weren't the massive ocean swells of the west coast, generated over hundreds of uninterrupted kilometres in the Pacific Ocean.

I loved seeing the water from every window in the large three-storey house, one of the old-timers with a fireplace (no longer in use), high ceilings and grand views. There is something to be said for unimpeded ocean views on a barren island with one brave tree glimmering with Christmas lights.

Seamus, Jeff and I talked and talked, about our shared past, our separate pursuits in the present and what the future might hold for each of us in best- and worst-case scenarios. As for myself, I was trying to write jolly, non-inflammatory, i.e., no mention whatsoever of the intended de-staffing of lighthouses on both coasts, puff pieces about the lightkeeping life with a focus on food and gardening, as well as *The Lighthouse Cat*, a picture book in honour of our old Woodycat. No luck with any of it except for more nice rejection letters to add to my collection. I rewrote my entire *Odyssey* novel in order to meet a contest deadline, a useful goad to getting rewrites done. No joy there either. I kept working on my magical hat novella throughout. "Patience, polish, persistence," I declared, my writing mantra courtesy of John Newlove, and hoped 2010 might be a breakthrough year. We all raised a toast to it.

We are a tightly bonded family, for whose closeness and affection I am so grateful. The paradox of parenting is that the ultimate result of doing a good job is that your children will flourish without you, claim their full-fledged independence and fly away. We are blessed in that Seamus is very caring and articulate, and while he is more than competent at looking after himself, he is also kind enough to stay in touch with us, his wayward, adventurous parents.

But all too soon it was time to pack up and clean as our twelve-day stint neared its end. We always try to leave a place as tidy as or even tidier than we found it—as one O.W.L. says, it's time to polish the doorknobs. Bonus: my Dutch genes kick in when I clean. I liked being able to leave the house sparkling, a thank-you for spending a quiet and lovely time in such a grand old-fashioned Christmas card house.

My last weather report from Entrance Island was at 2130, January 3, 2009, checking the sky (partly cloudy) and the waves (one-foot chop) with the anemometer giving an accurate account of a northwest wind blowing six knots under a nearly full moon. There was a blue moon late this December, and while gazing at it I hoped that next year at this time, Jason or another lightkeeper would be puzzling over the vagaries of weather observations from this same high deck. I hoped they, too, would smile when the gut-sick groans and throat-clearing harrumphs of the sea lions floated up to their

Relief work on Entrance Island is over and lightkeepers wait for the helicopter to land.

ears. I hoped someone would climb the tower stairs at 0415 to wipe down the excessive condensation on the lighthouse cupola windows, so the light would flash clearly and safely, like Jeff did so many early mornings during our stint.

Automation would mean no round-the-clock human beings on site to ensure the physical plant was working and the light was flashing so mariners and aviators could count on it when they needed it most. Who would tell the pilots that fog had moved in fast to smother the harbour and was so thick it was impossible to see the city lights? Who would hear yells in the fog and then make out an overturned boat or kayak? As we prepared for the helicopter to take us back to Lennard Island Lightstation, I hoped there would still be a Christmas on Entrance Island in 2010, with human beings to wave at seaplanes that waggled their wings in response.

If the proposed lightstation de-staffing announced in September was a trial balloon, it was popped from coast to coast, noisily and repeatedly. Lightkeepers were getting vociferous support from mariners, aviators and members of the public, like hikers who'd been helped with lightkeeper assistance on the West Coast Trail and hypothermic kayakers who'd been rescued by the lightkeepers of Trial Island. The minister of fisheries and oceans requested a comprehensive report on the additional contributions made to the public by lightkeepers, to be undertaken by a standing committee of senators. No lightstations would be closed until the report was delivered and considered by elected politicians. The introduction to the senators' report underlines the reaction of the user groups and stakeholders to the announcement:

> *Reaction to the plan was extremely negative. No formal review or consultation had taken place with user groups or stakeholders who responded by flooding DFO with letters voicing their staunch opposition, including the Union of BC Municipalities and the Federation of Canadian Municipalities, which voted unanimously in favour of a resolution calling "on the Prime Minister to cease all efforts to de-staff lightstations and instead commit to maintaining lightstation staffing levels indefinitely, in order to ensure the safety of the working and travelling public and the vibrancy of the growing coastal community.*

All the time and expense lightkeepers had put into getting internet reception to our remote stations was also paying off, big time. United and well-informed we stood. We had stalwart union representation, groups like the Georgia Strait Alliance to help—who represented fifty user groups as well as individuals, for a total of 150,000 mariners—and retired lightkeepers with immense political savvy, like Jim Abram from Campbell River, doing battle for us. Along with astute investigation and questioning from senators like Newfoundland's Bill Rompkey, Quebec's Roméo Dallaire and BC's Nancy Greene Raine. Blessings on all their fair heads.

In the end, the news was very good indeed, thanks to their December 2010 report, *Seeing the Light: Report on Staffed Lighthouses in Newfoundland and Labrador and British Columbia.* Their recommendation not to close Canadian lightstations en masse but to consider closures on a case by case basis, and only after thorough consultation with all stakeholders, would be respected by the minister and her colleagues on March 23, 2011.

And thus it was to be a Merry Christmas and Happy New Year to all, especially all lightkeepers and soon, in the years that followed, citizens whose lives were saved by lightkeepers at Entrance Island, Cape Beale, Chatham Point and Chrome Island. The report stressed the importance of the many tasks lightkeepers still perform, despite having so many responsibilities, training and key items of equipment, like station boats, removed over the decades. As the report stated:

> For decades, senior CCG managers have questioned the value of staffed lighthouses. It is an issue that just does not seem to ever go away. On both coasts, participants in our discussions expressed deep frustration about this situation. Some people we spoke to in British Columbia said that it was the fourth time they had appeared before a committee to fight to keep people "on the lights." The matter is important to the users of lighthouse services, to the Coast Guard, and to the lightkeepers themselves.

And then, on the political and ethical crux of the matter:

The value of lives saved by lightkeepers is greater than any savings resulting from de-staffing.

What I inevitably think about when someone's life is saved at sea, especially the life of a young teen or child, is that perhaps the person who will find the cure for a terrible disease or the future inventor of some marvel to ease suffering was just saved. It's a big deal—at any age—to get a second chance at life. We've lost so many brilliant people to wars and diseases on this earth already. Why not celebrate the lucky ones who are saved and honour those among us who get into their lifeboats, ambulances and lightstation boats to do the right thing?

THIRTEEN

The Cautious Mussel-Pickers Kouta

This month has an "r" in it
so we venture forth;
rockbound quarry clings, silent.
We clutch plastic bags.

Slow Food, Hot Oven

I WILL NEVER GET USED TO DUCKING AND WALKING UNDER THE BLUR of deadly helicopter blades. This is a good thing. A high school friend of mine, a pilot barely in his twenties, died on a northern mountainside because he forgot the rules. There are horror stories of absent-minded people nearly decapitating themselves by failing to notice they are walking downhill toward the chopper, oblivious to the frantic eyes and hand signals of the pilot, with the machine's high-decibel *whump-whump* growl muffled by earplugs, their eyes elsewhere, their brains likewise, disengaged... Well, you know where we're headed with that image. So it's a healthy survival response to break a light sweat and duck way down even when there are several metres of clearance, and to avoid the tail rotor area entirely, it being smaller yet much closer and more lethal than the big blades whirling above.

This particular chopper finally arrived on Lennard Island three days late with our month's worth of groceries, including the official Thanksgiving turkey. Dense fog and non-stop drizzle had obscured our helipad two days in a row but now we scrambled for earplugs and ran to welcome the red Bell 212 scooting toward us over the drifting fog patches. Our little John Deere tractor and wagon unit was ready to receive box after box of dry, canned, frozen and most precious of all, fresh, perishable foods.

The helicopter wobbled a little with thirty-knot winds swirling around it but the pilot brought it down neatly on our circle of green turf and white mussel shells. With the rotors still running, we formed a small chain gang and quickly stacked the boxes into the wagon. Then I handed over chocolate chip and dried cranberry cookies for the pilot and engineer before we got ourselves and our wagonload of groceries well out of the way for liftoff, waving as the chopper hovered overhead and then veered off to the northwest. One lightkeeper always stays to watch the helicopters take off safely. Two special fire extinguishers are within eight seconds' reach, in the fuel shed and engine room respectively.

Grocery day is a mini-Christmas on the lightstation, with the joys of special menu items (fresh mushrooms! lemon gelato! kiwi fruit!) mitigated by the odour of elderly sole fillets that have been in and out of the cooler at the Coast Guard base and the helicopter itself over the past three days. Our personal shoppers at Thrifty Foods in Victoria receive our emailed orders and do their best but sometimes boxes have to be consolidated and repacked at the Coast Guard base. This time our bags of fresh cranberries ended up in another lightkeeper's order and the cat food cans contained chunks of mystery meat in glutinous gravy, instead of food thoroughly disguised as pâté, which is what our seventeen-and-a-half-year-old feline vehemently preferred. Thanks to a thoughtful colleague, the crucial Thanksgiving cranberries were eventually rerouted to us, along with a bottle of Vancouver Island bigleaf maple syrup, a thank-you gift from another keeper for Jeff's internet problem-solving.

Then, woe is me: I made the unhappy discovery that someone had amalgamated the fresh and freezer boxes. A large bag of spuds had ended up in the mix. Nine potatoes survived, insulated by their Yukon Gold brethren. I monitored them daily to make sure we had solid spuds for Thanksgiving dinner's *de rigueur* garlic mashed potatoes. The spongy, smelly frozen ones went, with regrets, to our compost bin.

Dinner that night was baked sole, stuffed with sautéed onions, garlic, spinach and mushrooms, and a dollop of cream cheese, accompanied by wild and long-grain brown rice and a good salad with several kinds of lettuce and yellow cherry tomatoes from our greenhouse, chives from the herb garden, some store-bought artichoke hearts and a whole avocado rescued from the perishables in the very nick of time. *Salut!* TGIF! We toasted our hard work in the week past—the hours spent maintaining eleven buildings, changing the oil on the duty engine, fixing the finicky weed whacker, all of it. Plus the delayed yet ultimately successful arrival of our month's worth of groceries.

Now, the pantry shelves were stocked, the fridge was packed and the freezer was three-quarters full. We freeze all our dairy items: milk, blocks of cheese, and containers of feta, butter and cream cheese, to no ill effect. I am wary of freezer burn and wasted food so I date every package. Bad flying weather can strand our groceries as long as five days, our benchmark to date. So our pantry always has canned and dry beans, dried pastas and canned pasta sauces, several kinds of flour and rice in bins, my garlic dill pickles (and a mouth-puckering experiment with kelp pickles one year), several kinds of homemade jams and jellies, a variety of grains and, most crucially, bags of coffee beans specially ordered from Pistol and Burnes, a Vancouver wholesaler with wonderful coffee. Loose-leaf teas ordered from Murchie's Teas & Coffee are also must-haves and easily ordered from their website. Life, we decided long ago, is too short for bad coffee and weak tea!

We also supplement store-bought food with our garden and greenhouse produce and Jeff's growing success in his rowboat, at the end of a fishing pole (halibut, rock and green ling cod, coho salmon), and with Dungeness crab from our crab traps. Cooked crab freezes well in the shell for up to six months and Jeff makes melt-in-your-mouth crab cakes to live for.

Early in our posting to Lennard, we paddled our kayaks over to Mackenzie Beach one fine Saturday. Then we walked half a kilometre inland and discovered the Wildside Grill in Beaches Plaza on the highway south of Tofino, a funky outdoor restaurant with very good food. We found out we could buy quantities of frozen whole and filleted salmon and stripe and spot prawns as well as piping hot halibut burgers and shrimp baskets from the co-owner. Jeff Mikus is a long-time fisherman who catches seafood for the area's top restaurants and resorts. We are more than happy to fill our kayak holds with his frozen, pristine wild seafood and paddle it home to our own freezer just half an hour away.

Compared to lightkeepers in the century before us, who had groceries delivered by boat two or three times a year and who depended heavily on their gardens, the sea and hardy livestock to survive, we are mighty fortunate. When I think of those lightkeepers and their families, who waited for weeks and months for the grocery ship, who then slaughtered the last chicken and ran down the last scrawny goat, who mixed cornstarch and water to feed their

Caroline and Jeff land their kayaks on Mackenzie Beach. *Photo by Seamus Woodward-George*

children and other true horror stories of near-starvation on the lights, I count my blessings and do my utmost not to waste a scrap of food.

I am rediscovering my inner domestic goddess out here on the lights, on this little island surrounded by jagged reefs, relentless North Pacific swells and blustering gales. At this very moment, a batch of fermenting biga, an Italian sourdough bread starter, bubbles slowly in our fridge. There are twenty containers of frozen blackberries in the freezer from our thorny and productive wild bushes, which Jeff has thinned and pruned and staked and roped into a semi-domestic state. This year, I made two batches of spicy blackberry-peach jam, another batch of blackberry jelly and I will likely make more jelly out of the frozen berries during the housebound days of winter storms ahead. We'll add the berries to apple crisp, bumbleberry bars and fruit smoothies too. Jeff has just tried his hand at blackberry mead and now we patiently wait and hope for quaffable results. Some years the rain and the fog conspire to turn the entire blackberry crop into mildewed sour lumps so we make the most of the years when the sun shines and the rains arrive at just the right time to give us wave after wave of sweet-tart blackberries half the size of my thumbs.

Meanwhile, I make all our breads and pizza dough from scratch, favouring French bread, onion-rye bread and Italian sourdough: pagnotta, ciabatta and focaccia breads. Then I make various fruit squares that travel well and about six different kinds of cookies. About 90% of the latter end up in the tummies of the Tofino lifeboat crews who deliver and receive our mail and the pilots and work crews who arrive by ship or helicopter to do necessary repairs on our equipment and buildings. It is just plain hospitable and a morale booster to make and serve good food, considering the weather we all endure in the course of our workdays.

Carmanah Point Lightstation is renowned for its authentic bowls of *caffe latte*, not to mention the delicious lemon pound cake made by Janet Etzkorn, which I sampled when we dropped in to deliver a scientist specializing in earthquakes one day. The baking lightkeepers along the BC coast always have delicious and nutritious muffins, squares and cookies to keep the blood sugar of the lucky recipients spiking on a regular basis. Joanne and Mark Tiglmann, Nootka's lightkeepers, serve up the best smoked salmon in the world to honoured guests. I believe rum is involved. Or smoked rum, I don't know, I was too addled by the divine pescatorian fare to get all the facts straight!

During the growing season, the lighthouse gardeners also hand out carrots, cucumbers, zucchinis, tomatillos, fresh herbs and other excess produce from our gardens. Thrifty and creative cooks pickle and can and jam and brine and smoke. As frequent relief keepers, Jeff and I have been the lucky recipients of their gourmet results, and Sylvia Hacking, Estevan Point's hard-working lightkeeper-gardener-cook, currently holds the virtual North Pacific Fall Fair Best in Show ribbons for amazing leek scape pickles, beet and horseradish relish, and orange and cranberry syrup. It's all very well to live on bannock and beans and the occasional wrinkled apple but physical and mental health rallies mightily with imaginative and tasty fare. Guaranteed. Camp cooks of the nation are nodding and thumping their spoons on counters even as I type.

A pilot who had dropped down to deliver some paint to us once told me afterwards that he'd forgotten to bring his lunch that day. The only food he ate were two of my pony hoof–sized oatmeal cookies, which sustained him. I told him if he was ever in a bind again to please let me know as I would gladly pack a proper lunch for him.

When the Coast Guard ships come in to refuel us or bring in a crew to inspect and maintain the winch and high line, I always offer fresh coffee and tea, plus cookies, muffins or cake. When it's an all-day job, like the quadrennial anniversary to inspect and/or refurbish every line and cable and bolt, I usually bring out a big cake on a covered glass pedestal, little plates and dessert forks, and a choice of cloth or paper napkins. Pottery and china mugs, honey, cane sugar, real spoons. Cream if we have it, virtuous, boring 2% if we don't. As I told a happy crew member digging in to the triple-decker carrot cake one year, it is very important to celebrate the finer things in life whenever we get the chance.

Flowers on the table. Good mugs and tea cups for company. Cloth napkins and tablecloths. I've never forgotten Dad saying how lovely it was to have tea

Caroline offers fresh coffee and baking to the ship's refuelling crew on shore. *Photo by Caroline Woodward*

served in real china tea cups by a gracious Peace River couple who lived in a two-room log house in the 1930s. Or the long hours Mom worked, cooking up huge pots of food and baking three kinds of pie for dessert for the eight-man threshing gang. My dad and our neighbours all pooled their labour, horses and equipment when the threshing machine was towed to each farm in turn. CBC Television actually came out and documented our farmers at work in the early 1960s, the last threshing gang in Canada still working with horses, the hay racks piled high with sheaves of grain. Then technology and progress arrived in Cecil Lake and everyone went into debt to buy their individual swathers and combines, and the co-operative way of life disappeared too.

The homestead where I grew up meant that grocery shopping trips to the local Co-op ten kilometres away were, at most, done once or twice a month, and to Fort St. John, forty winding kilometres away, perhaps once or twice a year. We used workhorses to farm the land and to travel to the store and the community hall until we bought a steel-wheeled John Deere tractor when I was six years old. Then we bought a 1953 Chevrolet car the following year. But the car wouldn't start at all during our frigid winters, even when we kept the battery warm inside the house. Worse, most of the time our access road to the main road was completely blocked with snow because the snow grader only plowed it out two or three times the entire winter. So we used our dependable, all-weather team of horses pulling a caboose or a sleigh to get to the Co-op, taking a dirt back road that was only passable to horse-drawn traffic. During spring runoff, the muddy season, we hitched the team up to a nimble Democrat buggy or the wooden-wheeled, spine-jolting wagon and off we went.

My mother, a city girl, came from a household with no oven and a two-burner hotplate. Bread, when it was available during the starvation years of World War II, came from a bakery, and fish was fried at the fishmonger's and picked up in a covered pot brought from home, a forerunner to takeout food. She learned to bake bread, taught by my father, in an oven fired by balky green poplar wood. She preserved all meats by canning them, including the venison we ate more than any other meat because it was free and there were plenty of deer. She also canned wild saskatoon berries, green beans, pickled beets and rhubarb in glass canning jars, or "sealers," during the years before electricity. We stored potatoes and other root vegetables in the cellar beneath our farmhouse. Electricity finally arrived in Cecil Lake in 1964–65, decades after most Canadians enjoyed it, as the W.A.C. Bennett Dam was being built on the Peace River.

In fact, I feel very lucky to have grown up in the 1950s and '60s, in an environment that was very much like the 1920s and '30s as far as technology and community entertainment were concerned. It has informed my writing, of course, as did the aural history interviews I recorded with Peace River farmers, nurses, teachers, bush pilots and river freighters in the mid-'70s and which are stored in the Royal BC Museum oral history archives. Their voices still resonate in my head while I go about my work as a lightkeeper, with these precious days to reflect on people and life, and with decades of journals and daybooks to finally reread.

My daily journal habit devolved into keeping daybooks during those hectic years when I felt like a human doing more than a human being. I kept putting off writing in my journal when I moved to the lighthouse, thinking my daybooks crammed with to-do lists and menu synopses and assorted other weather and activity notes would be a crutch I could lean on for the day when I might begin writing my memoir.

I should've known better. I kept a daily journal faithfully for the best part of twenty years and sporadic thematic (mothering, poetry) and literary story idea journals for another twenty years. The daybooks, jammed with busy directives, took precedence. What I forgot, amidst the procrastination, is that writing a daily journal is writing practice. The eye observes, the ear absorbs the sounds of all the elements, the body feels fatigue or pain or sheer bliss and contentment, the mind dances all over the place... writing daily is writing practice. When we retire or are kicked off the lights and I attempt to write in the midst of packing up and establishing another way of life, I cannot hope to spring forth with reams of eloquent, telling details and pithy philosophical wisdom, if any enlightenment actually occurred, based on cramped to-do notes in the daybooks I've accumulated. I'm back to writing in a journal, not daily, thanks to being busy living and working and writing other things, but it is a touchstone again, a place to talk to myself about what matters to me with no self-made critics snarking away on my shoulder. The writer Isak Dinesen (*Out of Africa*) said: "Write a little every day without hope and without despair." That's where the journal lives for me.

Speaking of living, I had absolutely no intention of going "back to the land" when I left the homestead in the Peace for balmy Vancouver to attend university, but here I am, more than forty-five circuitous, adventurous years later. I'm living and working on a rocky, forested island tending a greenhouse and planning next spring's gardens. And writing nearly full-time.

I'd been warned by another lightkeeper that our diesel generators made the ovens run hot and the clocks run fast and she was absolutely right. My oven was reliably fifty degrees Fahrenheit hotter than the dial would indicate except when there was a heavy draw from other buildings on the station. Then the oven temperature behaves more accurately. This means taking due diligence when delicate shortbread or a whole baked salmon is underway. We had an ancient electric stove to begin with, too, so this variance added a wee frisson to culinary experiments. The elderly stove shorted and sparked in a disconcerting fashion during our second year in the assistant's house and after I discussed the symptoms with Ernest the Electrician, it was promptly replaced with a new stove that does not have the mood swings that the old beast did, which I appreciate.

Back when we used to camp in Valhalla Provincial Park, when Seamus was young, I created menus very carefully so there were kid-friendly snacks and a good variety of camp stove meals, and to ensure we had all the ingredients on hand for the days or glorious weeks we spent running wild. From these original menu and ingredient lists, which I saved in my recipe files (paper is my curse and my salvation), have come our lighthouse menus. They are especially useful when we do relief stints elsewhere. Now I have one-week, two-week, one-month and beyond menus and lists of ingredients, as well as notes about kitchen implements. I know that all across Canada and Alaska there are northern cooks in mining and oil and gas drilling camps, isolated ranch and farm women, and especially cooks in coastal air- or water-access-only camps and First Nations villages who do exactly what I do with shopping lists and menus. We have to keep bodies, minds and hearts in excellent working order out here.

During one memorable grocery order, delayed five days by nasty November weather, we were astonished to find at least three times as many brown mushrooms as we'd ordered. They were fulsome cremini beauties but they were aging before our very eyes. As well as mushrooms on and in everything we ate for the next two days, I made no less than two kilos of mushroom soup, blending the dried shitakes I always have on hand with the wizening fresh excess before me. Into the freezer in recycled plastic tubs went the soup, with my careful instructions in laundry marker as to how much sherry and sour cream had to be added for a deluxe lunch or dinner.

Jeff and I have at least forty cookbooks and are compulsive recipe clippers and internet recipe sleuths as well. We both love to cook, though I tend to do more of it—he has the permanent position and I work relief so I have more time. He is the king of salsas, curator of crab cakes, the master of pastas and the award-winning purveyor of chili, to note just a few of his culinary accomplishments. Best of all, he happily and meticulously washes dishes, which I relinquish any responsibility for when I'm doing the cooking. As with our early bird and night owl biorhythms, the cooking and washing division of labour adds to our compatibility checklist.

Even when I'm doing full-time relief shifts as an assistant lightkeeper, I can time the kneading sessions of bread production between my weather reports every three hours and work the five-hour process in around my outdoor maintenance tasks. I can mow the lawn or paint many metres of metal railings with Coast Guard red enamel and know that the slow cooker is doing a fine job on the kidney bean and kielbasa dinner I started in the morning. Just before dinnertime, one of us can quickly chop a coleslaw salad and reheat a rice pilaf.

I routinely make double recipes of entrees in order to freeze at least one meal and have a good portion ready for the next day's lunch as well. On those days when we come indoors stumbling with fatigue, yanking off workboots, coveralls or soaking wet rain gear, to stand under a blasting hot shower and emerge clean, tired and absolutely ravenous, how good it is to wolf down a spicy bowl of homemade mulligatawny soup, followed by steamed broccoli with lemon butter and sautéed almond slivers, and a baked salmon filet with a teriyaki, balsamic vinegar and maple syrup marinade, all prepped in advance. If there's room left for Jeff's sublime apple and salal berry crisp, topped with my homemade yoghurt, we'll dig into it, moaning gratefully with every second spoonful.

This is not to say that we've given up dinners consisting of nachos, popcorn or homemade dill pickles with cheese and crackers. Far from it. My soulmate's major food groups include chips, salsa, wine gums and any form of chocolate. I am partial to good cheeses from Vancouver Island artisans and the gamut of blue cheeses from sublime Cambozola to Old Socks, a.k.a. Gorgonzola. Tubs of feta are a must-have for my nettle or spinach spanakopita and for Jeff's pizza toppings. We order creamy little rounds of Boursin every single month, our most-beloved appetizer treat. My mouth is watering as I type and it's not the dinner hour yet. But it is nearly time to go to our gym in the former engine room and virtuously work out so that we can eat all this great food and not resemble Steller sea lions. Or California ones either.

I enthusiastically endorse the concept of eating and drinking less by eating and drinking better (although like Mae West, we all know too much of a good thing can be wonderful) and buying locally from real farmers—i.e., organic, ethical, non-GMO producers of food. So it means we order free-range, organic Vancouver Island farm eggs and pay an extra dollar a dozen. The eggs we buy are not only hen-friendly but taste ten times better. Likewise our own fresh tomatoes, English cucumbers, cilantro, basil and tomatillos from the greenhouse, or the flash-frozen sockeye salmon filets from our fisherman friend. Ditto for belonging to the Tofino Ucluelet Culinary Guild, which brings in top quality Peace River lamb, Okanagan dried cherries, Fraser Valley hazelnuts and much, much more for its members, who range from regular, reasonably inspired cooks like myself to the amazing chefs who work as professionals in village restaurants and the resorts along the ocean everywhere in between.

The easiest form of protein for us is to head out, as we did yesterday afternoon in our gumboots, wearing sturdy gloves, to pry mussels off the reefs. We have literally tens of thousands of California mussels within easy access on our rocks and reefs at Lennard Island. California mussels live from California to Alaska in the intertidal zones of the West Coast as they can withstand the storms and big surf much better than the indigenous blue mussel, which prefers calmer, deeper waters. We can pick all the mussels we need within five minutes of leaving our porch.

Back in the kitchen, I pour a cup of clam juice, some clippings of fresh thyme, a cup of white wine, a quarter cup of minced yellow onion or three shallots and two minced cloves of garlic plus a bay leaf into a large pot and simmer them for five or ten minutes. Then I dump in thirty or forty scrubbed and de-bearded mussels (Jeff's job at the sink while I zip around collecting fresh herbs and mincing members of the onion family) and cover. Steam the whole lot for seven minutes then ladle the mussels with half-opened shells into waiting bowls and whisk a handful of just-clipped Italian flat-leaf parsley and a couple of tablespoons of unsalted butter into the broth until the butter melts. Pour broth over each bowl. There you go. Easy-peasy Mussels Meunière you didn't have to pay an arm or a leg for, much less fly to Belgium. Dunk the broth with peasant-friendly hunks of freshly baked bread for a fast and delicious feast. I just wish we both liked mussels a wee bit more than we actually do, truth be told, and I often think of stories about stormbound Scottish islanders who had to eat so many mussels their skins turned pale orange. But we do manage a feast of them at least once a month during the winter, when there is less danger of red tide or other paralytic shellfish contamination.

We envy the lightkeepers with easy access to spot prawns the most. We would do almost anything for prawns or scallops. Almost.

Lightkeepers elsewhere certainly do well if skilled with a fishing rod, having their own boat and a safe dock in all seasons at which to tie it up. They can enjoy premium quality seafood with smokers, canners and vacuum-packing equipment to preserve a good variety of their catches. We do have crab traps and easy access to Dungeness crabs in the calmer summer months and for this treat, we are also the envy of other lightkeepers.

In November and December, most lightkeepers get into serious baking mode and spend many hours creating seasonal specialties in order to give most of them away. I was advised of this tradition and given estimates of amounts per box per outlet, thirty of this and sixty of that. I was terribly worried I'd let our island down if I made less tasty or fewer treats than people were accustomed to getting. But my labour-intensive gingerbread person cookie results were so large and time-consuming that the numbers quoted would not work unless I spent a solid week making and decorating the smirking little SOBs. Then I came to my senses and realized some people made clever

Jeff tries his hand at fishing in Nootka Sound. No luck but it's lovely out on the water on this sunny January day. *Photo by Caroline Woodward*

decorative variations of the same cookie recipe, i.e., icebox cookies, each one about the size of my gingerbread arm or half a leg, and unless I wanted to start a gingerbread person factory, I had to stop fretting and apply common sense. I tweaked a rum ball recipe, which is now renamed in honour of the most appreciative recipients: Tofino Radio Rum Balls. I do love baking and trying new things, like authentic Viennese stollen, a bread recipe from a writer friend. But one O.W.L. grew so tired of this tradition that she ordered large flats of date squares from Costco one year. Bada bing, bada boom, cheap and cheerful and best of all, done in one hour flat of cutting and repackaging, not twenty or thirty hours of slaving away over five gift boxes. Food for future thought on my part.

FOURTEEN

Crow Vendetta Renga

Now they dive-bomb me
when I work in my garden.
Hitchcock comes to mind…

Beady-eyed adversaries
take aim: foul ammunition.

Aha! *they cackle*
What a putz, a pushover.
Let's crap on her plants!

Unfazed by stones that fall short,
these crows jeer, "We'll be back!"

Dirt, Dough or Diesel

I KEEP MY CENTURY-OLD WEDDING RING, WITH ITS TWO PEARLS AND dainty diamond in a rose-gold band, handed down from Jeff's great-grandmother, and my twenty-fifth anniversary silver Tsimshian ring with two eagles (eagles mate for life) in a small wooden box the majority of the time. My hands are immersed in dirt, dough or diesel far too often to risk damaging them. I buff them up and wear them when we head Outside for holidays or I go out to work as a writer.

The stink of diesel, oil and helicopter fuel is just part of the workday's ambience while we are checking the engine room, tanks and fuel lines, grabbing freight from the helicopter with rotors running or wiping down the duty engine and the floor if it's really snotting oil all over the place, which is a safety hazard. Then there is transferring diesel fuel to the domestic tanks, gassing up the tractor and the lawn mowers with regular gas and other pearl-dissolving tasks. Better to clip my nails as short as possible and safeguard my heirloom rings for special occasions.

As for dirt, gardening, like cooking, is a passion of mine. And thankfully it is a valuable hobby out on the lights. Nearly every station has a greenhouse and a garden, although they vary widely in size and ambitious scope. If keen gardeners move on, and the new keepers aren't interested or knowledgeable, a station's gardens will quickly revert to rainforest jungle as the blackberry brambles, salal, creeping buttercup, cow parsnip and other wild plants move in on choice soil nutrients in mere months. If we have committed to doing a lot of summer relief work elsewhere, I'll just plant fall garlic and several beds'

Caroline pumps fuel from the Tidy Tank to the domestic tank on Quatsino Lightstation.

worth of potatoes and some salad vegetables. I won't risk the greenhouse crops, which can be seriously set back by only one hot afternoon's worth of inattention, their withered blossoms the end of many months of nurturing from a tiny seed.

The one and only year we turned down some summer relief work in order to look after the garden was a disastrous year in the weather department, and therefore the garden. The Tofino fog moved in during early July, stayed for all of Fogust and didn't leave until mid-September. The temperatures only got up to 14 degrees Celsius outside while beaming on Port Alberni in the low thirties for weeks on end. Our plants screamed for heat and sun, and the root crops, Chinese veggies and salad crops grew to one centimetre high and then stopped, completely stunted, and eventually bolted, tiny heads of yellow flowers on micro-plants. I replanted some of them three times that summer, with the same dispiriting results. Jeff rigged up grow lights in the greenhouse to coax the English cukes and tomatoes to fruition. The sweet and hot peppers were impossibly delayed. Only the cilantro and basil in their protected pots in the greenhouse thrived. And kale. Kale is the quintessential West Coast superfood and reliable outdoor plant, bless its leathery little heart (and leaves).

The previous keepers on Lennard Island Lightstation were enthusiastic gardeners and left a perennial legacy of twenty-five beds filled with strawberries, herbs and flowers, a lily pond and two ancient gooseberry bushes. Everyone who had ever worked here said the same thing: wait until spring. Meaning the daffodils would be cheerful, I thought, but that doesn't even begin to describe what grows out here and lifts even the most moribund of spirits. I arrived in August so the orange crocosmia, white Shasta daisies, pale orange dahlias and dark pink fuchsia hedges were thriving everywhere, buzzing with at least three different kinds of bees, including the gardener's friend, the mason bee.

During my first fall on the island, I planted the large cement cold frame with three kinds of garlic after harvesting the crop of softneck red-skinned garlic bulbs left by the retired lightkeepers. I replanted the best bulbs of the legacy garlic too, as it was obviously productive and acclimated. I protected them all from the winter monsoons with old single-pane windows.

One spring I salvaged an old roof gutter made of tough plastic to start an early pea crop. I placed it in the unheated greenhouse in February, filled it with garden soil mixed with starter soil, which had lots of vermiculite and fertilizer, and planted the peas. In late March, when the plants were ten centimetres high, I "peeled" out the soil, which held together nicely thanks to the vigorous roots, and laid it down in a waiting trench in a garden bed. We had lovely sugar snap peas by May.

Plentiful fresh water is not as major an issue here as it is on several dry climate lightstations, but we do depend on rain filling the station's four cisterns. Chrome Island has a permanent desalinization set-up for potable water, like long voyage sailboats do, and it produces very fine drinking water. But the gardens at Chrome depend on rainwater too so barrels are strategically placed below the downspouts leading from the eaves around the greenhouse extension roof.

Each of the three houses on Lennard Island has a 22,700-litre cistern for personal use and the station has one large stand-alone cistern with an 80,000-litre capacity. This cistern was built in 1904 and is, along with the radio building, the oldest construction on the island. The water is treated with chlorine but it is classified as non-potable, intended for gardens, fire suppression and as much of the pressure-washing as we can manage with the lengths of hose we have on hand.

The cement mix of the big cistern and the foundation of the radio building is a wonder. Crushed mussel shells, which would have been gathered on site, are clearly visible in the mix, and despite being 110 years old as I write, the cistern shows no sign of crumbling or cracking. This may have everything to do with experienced masons in the team building this station, tradesmen who knew exactly where to situate these large, load-bearing buildings and exactly how to mix long-lasting cement. At least four lighthouse towers have been built here, and the first five-ton lens, shipped over from England and hoisted up by block and tackle to the top of the tower in 1904, was the largest on the BC coast at the time, with its twin installed at St. Catherine's Lighthouse on the Isle of Wight.

This island's parent material is made up of mussel shells, assorted granite boulders and rocks of igneous origin, and a thin, acidic skin of earth beloved by mosses. Very steep slopes and what I call abrupt hills are everywhere—think oversized hummocks or decomposing giant tree stumps—hence the necessity for building a land bridge to connect the houses and the key buildings. The land is shifting and slumping, however. Our boathouse's cement floor has buckled and cracked, slowly succumbing to gravity. Massive stumps of old-growth Douglas firs and cedars, now overgrown with honeysuckle, ivy or salal, remain as well, from when the first work crew cut all the big trees down. Local, reliable rumour has it that the initial work crew were given incorrect directions as to the proposed lighthouse site. Or they misinterpreted the correct directions. In any case, they chopped down the trees on the wrong side of the island first. The first-growth Douglas fir and cedar stumps throughout today's mature spruce grove offer mute but solid testimony to this account. When the error was pointed out to them, they set about chopping down all the trees on the other half of the island.

Nobody knows who brought the English ivy out to the lightstation to cover up the rubble and the ragged remnants of the original trees, but it deserves its reputation for strangling everything in its path. I make regular forays into the spruce grove with my secateurs to "girdle" the vines at a metre or so above ground. The diminished sunlight, thanks to the dense stand of spruce trees, merely slows the growth of this voracious and invasive plant. I don't mind if it covers up an ugly pile of old cement blocks but I do take exception to its boa constrictor habits with other plants and trees.

I am often reminded of the excursion Jeff and I once made to the Bernt Ronning Garden near Holberg at the northern tip of Vancouver Island when our ferry to Prince Rupert was delayed and we had a day to spare. Ronning was a Norwegian immigrant who worked as a camp cook, trapper and fisherman, having established his homestead at the end of the San Josef Wagon Road. This wagon trail was supposed to become the year-round road to the Danish settlement at Cape Scott but the provincial government of the day reneged on its promise, stranding those ill-fated pioneers with no timely or efficient way to get their dairy products to market.

Bernt Ronning and his brother Arnt cleared five acres of the rainforest and, possessed of a positively incandescent green thumb, Bernt grew monkey puzzle trees, daffodils, oaks, copper beech, varieties of bamboo, magnolias, rhododendrons and hundreds of other plants. He ran a mail-order business selling his seeds and cuttings, especially from the monkey puzzle trees, which are still some of the largest and oldest in BC. Bernt Ronning passed away in the 1960s and within a decade the rainforest reclaimed most of his garden. But then former lightkeepers Ron and Julia Moe became the caretakers of the property and as they cleared more and more of the terraces and meadows of indigenous vegetation, an astonishing variety of trees, shrubs and flowers reappeared. With the help of trained foresters and botanists, the Moes have identified such exotic plants as Swedish white balsam, golden yew and Japanese cedar. The garden is open to the public and is well worth the sixty-five-kilometre drive from Port Hardy, even just to see the greenhouse filled with pots of little monkey puzzle trees.

Inspired by these horticultural revelations, we have followed suit on Lennard Island. Jeff has taken the hedge trimmer to the rambunctious jungle and voila, the more we bushwhacked the blackberries and salal from what looked like nothing but cement retaining walls initially, the more we were rewarded with the sudden appearance of metre-high indigo delphiniums and Siberian irises, freed from the smothering green prison like sleeping beauties.

By digging out a thuggish bunch of Shasta daisies and using secateurs on overgrown ivy, honeysuckle and salal as well as a lot of moss, I've reclaimed borders and small terraces that then rewarded us with tiny spring bulbs like snowdrops and grape hyacinths, grateful for the daylight and the extra elbow room. There are secret gardens in the underbrush and swaths of flowers behind a thick hedge of salmonberries where excess roots and bulbs were moved, or maybe just tossed, by earlier lightkeepers. I am reminded of the eerily rapacious growth of the vines covering the palace of Sleeping Beauty. If we don't keep trimming and cutting back the rainforest jungle, I have no doubt the entire lightstation would be strangled by ivy, salal, creeping buttercup and blackberries within a decade.

We ration our water carefully as we are never sure how long the summer dry spells will last. We often need to use the water from our house cistern for its proximity to necessary tasks: pressure-washing, washing the engine room floor, flushing the boat motor's cooling system after every use and watering several garden beds near our house. We have a dehumidifier running in the basement and when it fills up, we dump the clean water into our washing machine or we give it to the lilac or the David Austin rose, both of which are planted in old mussel shell soil that drains exceedingly quickly. Beside the kitchen counter we have a large pail into which we drain our pasta and vegetable steamer water, cold tea, veggie scrubbing water, water from the salad spinner, the boiled eggs—in short, any excess water we use goes into the pail. We water the rose or the herbs or the strawberries nearby with it.

We gauge our toilet flushing habits accordingly and we don't let the tap run while we brush our teeth or wash our faces, all small conscious acts that add up to saving many litres of water every day. If we know there won't be a work crew or relief keeper using the crew house for months, we take our showers there and use the washing machine as well. It goes without saying that we shower in the navy way during the dry season: use just enough water to get wet, turn the water off to lather up with soap and shampoo, and then use just enough water to rinse off.

What *is* an issue here on Lennard Island is soil contamination from a century's worth of lead paint, mercury, cadmium and chromium being blasted off the buildings and onto the land by relentless Pacific winds. The binder with the environmental assessment and maps in the radio room office showed us where the hot spots were and the news was not good for many of the garden beds. But we also learned about a soil remediation program for those lightstations with serious gardeners and we applied to be considered for the program. This would mean getting clean, screened topsoil, lots of it, and geo-textile cloth that blocks the uptake of heavy metals but allows water to drain through from the top down. We'd also get the hardware and untreated lumber with which to make new raised garden beds.

Our timing was perfect and our station was selected for a remediation project. We handled bag after two-hundred-kilo bag of topsoil in two separate helicopter sling operations. The topsoil was brought by truck to a Tofino location that was open enough for our helicopter to work safely. Crew there attached the bags to the dangling hook from the hovering chopper and minutes later, we unhooked each bag near the two main garden areas. Then we all worked on the arduous job of filling the boxes, a job meaning many, many wheelbarrow loads of dirt heaved into the wooden frames lined with geo-textile.

Meanwhile there were five large wooden compost bins already in place. The winter storms bring us vast quantities of seaweed, mostly kelp, which adds nitrogen to the garden beds and compost. Sadly, we cannot add our lawn grass clippings due to their heavy metal contamination. I toss in spent soil from the big pots we grow cilantro and basil and cherry tomatoes in, all kept in the greenhouse, but we don't even have leaves from deciduous trees to add as brown material either! A lightkeeper planted an oak tree down beside the helipad but it's in a red-circled hot spot too because the proximity of the engine room diesel exhaust and the prevailing winds have made the leaves toxic. It is a tall and lovely tree with so many leaves… sigh. But we do our best with what we have and I buy bags of steer manure as well as bone meal, Alaska fish fertilizer and other food for the land. We also make extremely stinky pails of nettle, comfrey and seaweed tea to use in diluted form, especially to spray directly on the tomatoes in the greenhouse. I have to hold my breath when I take off the lid and mix it up but the stuff works and it's free fertilizer so… I'll just keep using it, holding my breath for as long as possible.

During my Haida Gwaii adventure with the Book Ladies, we stayed in a sweet guest cottage beside Sitka Studio in Tlell. The owners had a very large unheated greenhouse built like a Haida longhouse where they grew vegetables of all kinds. There were tall outdoor beds made with split logs for strawberries, but inside the greenhouse grew all the members of the green salad family plus root vegetables, tomatoes, cukes and the squash fraternity. It was not hot and stuffy but a very pleasant temperature, given the northern latitude with its long hours of sunlight but cool summers, as well as hurricane-force winds and much, much rain.

Their wonderful greenhouse convinced me it could be done, as did the photograph album in our radio room documenting Tony and Margaret Holland's gardens (1974–96) and Kathy Doyle and Iain Colquhoun's further adventures in horticulture while tending the light (1998–2008). Both couples were avid gardeners and left a legacy of flowers, fruit, trees, ponds and hedges. I thank them for all their hard work and fine eyes for beauty year-round. Okay, maybe not so much for whoever planted the comfrey, the heal-all plant of the seventies, which I'm still doing battle with, and transforming into that smelly high potency nitrogen tea.

When I retired from my work, my colleagues apparently deliberated over whether to buy me a stunning piece of First Nations silver jewellery or a mighty generous gift certificate to Lee Valley Tools. Bless their dear heads, they made the right decision and I promptly ordered several heat-activated window openers for the greenhouse, which we already planned to double in size. With our fluky combo of sunshine and fog summers, these automatic windows are a disaster prevention work force all by themselves. We have the gas cylinder mechanism set to open once the interior of the greenhouse reaches 20C but even with both the door and two other windows open, it can reach 36C inside, becoming a hothouse. I use draped white remay cloth to protect the English cukes and tomatoes from burning up into brown crispy shreds. It's not a perfect system but with care and vigilance, it works.

I ordered enough plant starter flats to begin all my own transplants, all-weather labels, tomato cages, assorted clippers and hand tools, and other gardening gizmos. We also bought heavy-duty plastic for the greenhouse extension, and chicken wire and other must-haves from Tofino and Ucluelet hardware stores. Tony and Jeff did a boffo job on the greenhouse extension, including a potting bench, and Jeff built all kinds of trellis support systems for peas and beans, and the all-important bird and dog damage prevention systems. However I must do battle with onion root maggot and cabbage root maggot, new and troublesome invaders in the gardens.

In the new raised garden beds, I was keen to plant raspberries, blueberries, asparagus and all kinds of vegetables. I planted a Grandpa Sadler apple tree as well. The Ordinary Corner Nursery in Tofino was and is my go-to resource for garden seeds, supplies and advice, especially since owner Trina Mattson, also a garden columnist for *Tofino Time Magazine*, really knows which plants can withstand the wind, the rain, the salt spray and the foggy, dry summer seasons we live with here. These West Coast gardening conditions are the most challenging I've ever faced.

Some summers, I have had to admit partial defeat after I've replanted two or three times a spring only to have the summer fog block the sun for weeks on end. Then fox sparrows get under the chicken wire cages we've built to keep them out. They scratch like small wild chickens, destroying whole rows of tiny seedlings in minutes. Their relatives, the golden-crowned sparrows, migrate every spring and the alert gardeners on our ALN circuit try to warn each other of the northward advance of the destructive flying phalanx.

The Etzkorn family, our front line keepers at Carmanah, warn Lorraine at Pachena and Karen at Cape Beale and on up the circuit to me at Lennard,

Barred owl on the old swing set at Pachena Point Lightstation.

Sylvia at Estevan and Joanne at Nootka as the golden-crowned assholes (so renamed by one usually mild-mannered and soft-spoken lightkeeper via email, as we aren't allowed to curse on the ALN phone) take about a day to fly to each of our stations. Thus warned, we gardeners all fly around ourselves, checking for security breaches in our chicken wire cages and securing many metres of remay cloth (the most recommended choice of O.W.L.s for protecting tender crops from all kinds of marauders all season long) over our garden beds. These migrating sparrows are very hungry and they will lay waste to any unprotected seedlings as well as go after underground seeds. They are welcome to the worms in the lawns and the bugs on the ground but they are not welcome to our many hours of labour—and not inconsiderable sums of money—spent on getting a garden growing out here!

Speaking of pests, dozens of enormous banana slugs ooze into our salad beds, chomping and pooping as they go, no matter how many crushed egg-shells or copper wire circles I spread around the spinach, lettuce and sorrel, in particular. They chow down on tender young brassicas too but peppery arugula keeps them at bay, as do Italian endives (a bitter green member of the dandelion family) and Chinese mustard. We'd have to start a brewery to have enough beer to drown them all, a much-touted organic method of dealing with them in a place without garter snakes, a natural predator of slugs. Some years I must surrender, apply the beer internally to myself and buy Slug Bait, a commercial product that works for as long as water is kept off the pellets... so it's pricey and it's not perfect either.

Some dispirited coastal gardeners just chuck all vegetable dreams and grow what grows amazingly well, which are rhododendrons and weigela (beauty bush) and other easy-care flowering shrubs. There are five-metre-high pink rhododendrons thriving on Lennard Island, with several showing signs of age: mossy limbs and dwindling blossoms. I give the ailing ancient ones coffee grounds and even special fertilizer for acid-loving plants but I think they need a no-nonsense pruning. I will need to find out how to do this so as not to kill them off entirely. There's no nonsense and then there's cack-handed butchery.

Honeysuckle vines grow beside much of the land bridge and in spring, the fragrance is enough to stop anyone in their tracks for a fortifying sniff. The fuchsia hedges are fragrance-free but still a lovely sight and best of all, they bloom year-round just like the two-metre-high fuchsia hedges alongside the narrow roads of Ireland. The rufous and the less common Anna's humming-birds swarm these flowers, and the pink salmonberry flowers too.

Prairie denizens, Easterners and Maritimers unite and collectively roll their eyes when national TV does their annual hard news report in February about the flower count in Victoria. While less-fortunate Canadians are taking a rest from digging themselves out of snow banks and chiselling the nostricles off the ends of their rosy noses, they are forced to view some Tilley-hatted individual with an overbite blatting on about paperwhite narcissi and blah-blah-800,000 daffodils-blah-blah. Worse, all their gleefully retired pals on Vancouver Island and surrounding islands are now tweeting incessantly and Instagramming close-up photos of their purple and yellow anemones and lily of the blue what-nots, while faking sincere condolences about snowstorms happening in Calgary twelve months of the year.

I have joined the ranks of the bulb-besotted, although I try not to be as insufferably smug about it, just privately as grateful as all get-out. When I first saw drifts of snowdrops under a free-standing fuchsia shrub, I blinked. I thought we'd had an overnight skiff of snow and low banks of it were left to melt there. But no, Jeff had brushed back the ubiquitous salal and ivy at that very spot back in the fall and voila, there in hardy, porcelain beauty was our reward in January. The snowdrops bloom first and then it's a neck and neck race between the tiny purple and yellow anemones, a.k.a. crocuses. This is all very lovely on the domestic front but for me there are still no flowers signi-fying spring as beautiful a sight, or with as subtle and sweet a fragrance, as the millions of pale purple prairie crocuses on the breaks of the Beatton River in May. And lilacs. Lilacs are the very essence of spring to a northerner and prairie person and while the hardy fragrant beauties manage to thrive in forty below, they struggle to grow on Lennard Island due to its acidic soil, so I apply lime three or four times a year to coax blooms out of the one lilac bush we have.

The next wave of flowers appears on the inelegantly named pigsqueak plants (*Bergenia ciliata*) usually in February, with long-lasting, two-toned, odour-free pink flowers. They do have glossy thick green leaves, and if they are vigorously rubbed with bare hands, a most satisfying squeaking noise is produced. They often make me think of the fun lighthouse kids raised here must have had with them, in the same way that Dad taught us how to produce a discordant shriek by blowing on a blade of grass trapped vertically between two thumbs.

Then we witness what other keepers told us about before we arrived on Lennard: thousands of daffodils, dark yellow, double-frilled, two-toned striped, single fluted, pale yellow, tall, short and in-between, in all the long borders on the station and most spectacularly in the stone-walled terraces descending between the cement steps to our house and the land bridge. Around the lily pond, filled with braying Pacific tree frogs all doing Pavarotti imitations in order to get laid (i.e., attract mates to propagate the species, for the Prudish, Faux-Scientific Reader), as well as blushing ivory water lilies, were dark purple primroses and yellow water irises. The daffodils were soon interspersed with the purest blue colour of agapanthus, a.k.a. Lily of the Nile, and elsewhere popped up fragrant pink and blue hyacinths, swaths of purple grape hyacinths, lovely blue scilla and dark pink rhododendrons. Hard on their heels came the hardy white Shasta daisies, tiny pastel English daisies all over the lawns, pure yellow *hypericum calycinum*, or St. John's wort, two deep red peony bushes and dozens of pink and purple lupins. Wave after wave of colour—cheerful yellow elecampane, pink hydrangeas and red, pink and white astilbe—surround the lily pond by midsummer. Purple phlox, mauve California lilac, English lavender, tiger lilies, pale orange dahlias and bright orange crocosmia bloom throughout the rest of summer and fall.

When we came out to the West Coast, I brought with me several tubers of pale yellow irises, which I first found in a ditch in the abandoned West Kootenay mining camp of Retallack. These lovely old-fashioned flowers had lined the front of our Motherlode Bookstore in New Denver. When we moved to Comox on Vancouver Island, I took several tubers with me and planted them there, and later, moved some to Union Bay. Now they grow beside our front doorstep along with a resident Oriental poppy, which is an unusual and gorgeous pale purple colour. I am trying to dig out comfrey and a mountain ash tree from the same spot so the irises and poppy, as well as some tall pink Japanese anemones, will face less burly competition for water and soil nutrients.

Every year I've lived on Lennard Island I have managed to collect and trade seeds and plants with other lightkeepers and Tofino gardening friends. Thanks to helicopter pilots and ship's crews passing along boxes of seedlings and roots from one station to another, and kind donations while off doing relief work elsewhere, we now have a thriving pot of rosemary from Carmanah Point beside our back door, lady's mantle, French tarragon and wild sheep sorrel from Chatham Point, paperwhite narcissus from Nootka, seven different colours of hollyhocks grown from seed saved from the hundreds growing on the banks of Chrome Island and tall pale pink Japanese anemones from Estevan Point. A little holly plant was rescued from a runner sent out by a tree completely surrounded by willows at Quatsino. Our hardy everbearing strawberries have gone out to anyone who will have them and now thrive at high altitude in the arid south Okanagan at my sister's house as well as the soggy, foggy West Coast conditions of Nootka Light and Quatsino Light. But the best flower is saved for last.

The David Austin tea rose, espaliered against our kitchen wall and facing southeast, was planted by now retired lightkeeper Iain Colquhoun, who left good instructions as to its pruning and watering. I've never met Iain but I could tell by his instructions that the rose meant a lot to him. I've always wanted a garden with roses and asparagus, both signifying stability and longevity. Well. I'd never pruned a rose before but that's why God invented YouTube and Google. Not to mention veteran gardeners who have contributed to the shelf full of gardening books now in our home library.

This rose blooms three times a year with over one hundred incredibly fragrant and beautiful pink roses in May, July and September, with roses often lasting on the branches well into November. I prune it during the first hard winter frost and I've learned that we may only get one good deep frost so when it happens, I drop everything else I'm doing and get out there on the stepladder with my secateurs. We water it faithfully, clean up all the volunteer lunaria (silver dollar) plants and any weeds and debris around it in the fall, and we feed it store-bought rose food and chopped banana peels for potassium, which it apparently appreciates. Every year it grows more than five metres high, up beside our kitchen window, no matter how much tough love I've put into pruning it. Having a hard day? Nose in rose will cure all ills. I email Iain and Kathy photos of the current year's blossoms, to let them know we are taking good care of the rose they had to leave behind, as we will have to do ourselves some sad day.

By November, though, I want the benevolent tyranny of the garden to cease. Winter is for my writing, for the long stretches of uninterrupted time that I need. Summer is so distracting and demanding and by that, I don't mean just the garden work. I mean the rare and perfect dry weekend days with no to low winds and no fog, days ideal for kayaking around Wickaninnish Island or over to Vargas Island to visit with our friends there, or across Templar Channel to buy *The Globe and Mail* and the *Vancouver Sun* and some treats at Beaches Grocery—a chance to join the laid-back land of happy tourists for half an hour.

During the spring and through the fall, unless I have a major book deadline, I manage to write in my lighthouse journal, meet deadlines for book reviews or fiddle around with drafts of children's book projects. I also enjoy writing Japanese form poems—short pieces for my commensurately short summer attention span, because in those fleeting days of warmth, there are limited opportunities to get out on the ocean in our kayaks. One hour on the water is worth four on land… and we may only get a handful of those days so we leap at every chance.

But first there is finishing the harvest and the fall planting of garlic and getting the purple sprouting broccoli, cauliflower and kale into winter beds. I transfer the hardy winter lettuce to the cold frame and hope the sorrel, arugula, Italian endive, Swiss chard and tah tsai will survive to perk up our mid-winter meals. By this time the freezer is stocked with small plastic tubs of pesto: cilantro, dill, basil, arugula and herbes de Provence, a five-herb blend of Italian parsley, basil, thyme, oregano and rosemary. Bags of wild spring nettles are already frozen, waiting to be transformed into Jeff's vegetarian lasagna and my spanakopita and gnocchi. Fava beans and peas are blanched and frozen in meal-sized quantities, as well as many bags of blackberries, strawberries, salal berries and raspberries. The garlic is hanging in braids in the coolest, darkest spot in our basement and below them our potatoes are put to bed for the last time in plastic totes filled with dry potting soil, where they will last for months.

Winter, bring on your worst. If we are abandoned entirely by the world, as happens in the novel set in the year 2060 I am now writing draft four of, we can survive on what we have put away and by jigging for rock cod and

Caroline happily runs out to get some greens from the garden at dinnertime.

venturing out in the rowboat to try our luck with any salmon, Dungeness crab or halibut still left in the ocean. I'm able to bring all the things I find fascinating about this natural world, finally, into my prose as well as my poems and children's stories. I happily research among our six bookshelves (described by several relief keepers as worthy of the Best Library on the Lights Award) and order more books from the indispensable mail-order service for remote readers offered by Vancouver Island Regional Library.

I decide my hardy fictional survivors of 2060 will need to emulate the Japanese and utilize tasty and nutritious seaweeds more often in their meals. I will develop milder brine for my next batch of kelp pickles and see if I can make a palatable batch of blackberry vinegar. We will wrench mussels off our reefs and forage for wild onions and delicate and delicious sea asparagus. It's all such interesting field research.

But for coffee, we'd have to roast wild chicory roots, which I plan to experiment with this summer. It may well prove to be my breaking point. Coffee is the last beloved inanimate item I would ever give up in this lifetime. But I write fiction! Fiction to the rescue! I will arrange to have a serendipitous stash of tea discovered in an abandoned boat by my shipload of survivors and then a ship's container of coffee beans, good dark roast ones, afloat near Haida Gwaii...

FIFTEEN

Ocean Thunder Kouta

Oceanic bombardment
this island's very bones vibrate
inside a giant's djembe
thumped relentlessly

Going Inward

Today, Sunday, I have the gift of insomnia. Again. Tired and wired. Worry has taken wing and is circling around my brain, unable to land or do anything but circle round and round. I look out our bedroom window and up at the tower. The bands of light are narrow and brisk and bright, not wide and slow and freighted with fog. I watch the steady revolving of the light and find the regularity of its multiple beams soothing. Comforted, I sink back down to meditate my way back to sleep.

The December storm has taken a breather and is simply showering us with mild bouts of rain. The day before we were pounded by ice pellets until the earth was white with them. The chilly wind kept them frozen all day and drove them in shallow drifts. The sound of the swell was like no other, a relentless, rhythmic push. Salt water bashed and broke against the black volcanic reefs around the island. Seething yellowed mounds of foam flooded through our channel and lunged over the final rock barrier, leaving salt spray hanging in the air high above. Spindrift, that lovely word for airborne seafoam, dropped in clumps all over our island while the salt spray adhered to every window, plank and leaf. We were forever cleaning our eyeglasses.

We hoped to leave in four days' time to spend Christmas with family in the Okanagan, our first Christmas away from the lights in six years, so the weather watch had begun. By that I mean we watched the marine forecasts for west and south coast Vancouver Island. Sea state was not an issue for helicopters, thankfully, but pilots only fly when they can see and when they aren't buffeted by gusting winds. So we hoped for a clear day, no fog, drizzle or heavy rain. We hoped for light winds, not high winds with vicious gusts. Also, no thunderstorms or water spouts. So much of our life is about the weather...

Late the previous night the northwest winds ramped up and shrieked and moaned and thumped around the island for hour after hour. Most of this I'm used to but the combination of the highest tides of the winter and winds of up to fifty knots created a rhythmic series of wallops in one of the island caves within earshot. Every few minutes there was a tremendous *whomp* as a swell surged into the narrow channel near us and boiled up high until it rebounded off the walls of the cave. The volcanic rock of our reefs is hard stuff but the force of the ocean scouring it like a relentless washerwoman attacking soiled linens with boiling water and a club has caused some erosion over the centuries.

This year it was very important for our family to be together because my funny, hard-working, far too young brother-in-law was suffering from Alzheimer's, and we all knew it could be the last "good" Christmas. Which turned out to be sad and true. My sister Mi, now my only surviving sibling

Waves break on the southeast corner of Lennard Island during a storm in January 2015.

of the original four in our family, has always been my closest family member. After this grim diagnosis, we began emailing each other at least once and sometimes three times a day, online support to augment the terrific neighbours and friends she already has. We are each other's no-nonsense reality checks and mutual cheerleading squad. I am proud of her career as a troubleshooting bank manager, the one sent in to fix flagging operations, like a bank where insider thieves were at work, or accounts were dropping like fall leaves. As with another smart cookie of my acquaintance who is a forensic accountant, I would love to ghostwrite both their stories, aiming for a bestseller in the financial thriller genre.

One of our in-jokes for decades has been: Don't die and leave me with the rest of them. We can make each other laugh so hard that we can't even catch our breath or make a sound. We tap into childhood goofiness and render each other giddy and helpless. Once I was driving and had to pull over so we could just howl with laughter and not bash into anyone else on the road. "Officer, I thought I would pee my pants and pass out simultaneously because I couldn't breathe. Because I was laughing so hard, she made me, so it's her fault. Honestly, we just drank one really good coffee each back in Princeton at that little café just off the highway."

Anyway, there would be many helping hands to lighten my sister's load as we all signed up in teams to be responsible for meals. Our plan was to drive to the Okanagan from Vancouver Island in a rented SUV jammed with four adults—Jeff, me, Seamus and his girlfriend, Georgina—plus Molly Brown, Christmas presents and winter wear. Oh, and cross-country skis and snowshoes.

The weather gods smiled on us. The helicopter landed safely and we flew up from our turf helipad and zoomed over the reefs where an eagle, inured to frequent helicopter visits, stayed put on the table rock facing the open Pacific. I turned to wave at the two lightkeepers now on duty who watched us for signs of anything untoward, and then I watched as the red roofs and white buildings, the raised garden beds and the greenhouse, and five large yellow fuel tanks beside our engine room shrank below us. The tower stood tall and the Canadian flag flew beside it. Then we were up and over the grey-green Pacific, flying south to Victoria, with mail stops at Cape Beale and Carmanah Point Lightstations.

I sat in the front seat beside Randy Meszaros, the pilot, draped in one of the silver tree garlands he had artfully placed in the passenger seat. We all waved at the lightkeepers who came out to handle the mail. Patti at Cape Beale touched her heart and waved back at us, her blue eyes and big smile expressing what we could not hear over the roar of the helicopter or through our earmuffs. Justine at Carmanah Point grinned as she reached in to pat Molly Brown in her crate and handed over her outgoing mail to Jeff, beside M.B. in the backseat. Our little pooch was all gussied up for Christmas with my sister's gift, an orange neckerchief from the SPCA in Zihuatenejo, Mexico, around her neck and her Mutt Muffs on her ears.

The drive was long and cramped, despite the mid-size rental SUV. I had presents piled all around my feet and I shifted my legs carefully. Our gear in the back was packed to the roof so we had to use our side mirrors exclusively. Winter driving is not a lot of fun at the best of times and we were out of practice. In fact, after several years of using it only a few times annually, we'd sold our little Echo to Seamus for a dollar. It was not happy being parked for months at a stretch, left to marinate in the salt air, the battery inevitably dead and the tires low in air whenever I needed to use it to get out to a writing gig. So now we make good use of city and regional bus systems, rent a car or get on a plane when we are out and about in the world. This time, given the winter luggage, the number of passengers and the dog, it was most sensible to rent a vehicle.

We've been able to arrange for Tofino lifeboat and helicopter transportation out to Lennard Island for most of our family members during the fair weather months, visits filled with feasts at the picnic table on the "lanai," which is actually our boat deck with a spectacular ocean view from on high. Free-form bocce games on the helipad, horseshoe tournaments in the pitch beside it, hikes around the island trail, heading out with fishing rods in the boat and exploring the beaches for exotic limpet and abalone shells among the plentiful mussel shells were all part of these wonderful reunions. My mom loved sitting on the bright red Japanese-style bench and looking at all the flowers. "It's like a park," she kept saying, beaming, so thrilled by her first ever helicopter ride, a five-minute hop from the Tofino Lifeboat Station.

But Christmas, Thanksgiving, Mother's Day, Father's Day and birthdays are special family occasions for us, as for most. Phone calls and emails and texts don't begin to compare to spending time face to face. Quantity time, as any sensible parent knows, leads to quality time. We can and do drop everything to be with family when there is a crisis. But when people are suffering through years of eroding health, that's when the tug to make family visits is strongest. Mi and I have made dozens of quarts of dill pickles and canned peaches together and in between sterilizing the sealers, blanching the peaches or scrubbing the cukes, we've solved more than a few of Life's problems. However, bucolic summer visits are not always possible if Jeff and I are both working, so the hazards and hassles of winter travel must be endured. Including the ferry crossing to the mainland, it takes us nearly eleven hours to arrive, unscathed, at their ranch-style home up high in the sagebrush hills of the Okanagan.

We cross-country skied and snowshoed for hours on the Nature Conservancy trail through a heritage ranch, mere minutes from their doorstep. We had two ecstatic dogs for company including Mi and Greg's Newfoundland-Pyrenees cross (our best guess as to Spikey Lee's parentage). Molly was experiencing snow for the first time. The theme for *Midnight Cowboy* came to mind, watching our shaggy muskox of a dog, like a canine Midnight Cowboy, finally getting to a place where the weather suited her fur. Greg was slower on the skis and needed more rests than usual but he loved the outing and the extra company.

We piled into the outdoor hot tub afterward and did our farm chores as well, packing wood to keep the heater belting out the BTUs indoors. Everyone pitched in to help with meals, which gave our homegrown Martha Stewart a break from looking after absolutely everything. I wished, oh these countless useless wishes, that I could be closer, to do more practical things to help her with respite care, but all I could do was send her loving emails and urge her to ask for more help and support, which was hard for her to do. Life deals us blows like this, so cruel and unfair. I remind myself: the ocean doesn't care. It is a force of nature. Waves roll in. Waves roll out. Life goes on. We must go forward and learn to allow our heavy hearts and grievous burdens to be buoyed by the kindness and helping hands of others.

I'm so glad we made the effort to spend that Christmas together, hellish though winter holiday travel inevitably is. It was hard to leave in the darkness of early morning, hard to wave goodbye to Mom, who thrives at family get-togethers, and to Mi and Greg, alone and fairly isolated in the country. I worried for them all, which is a futile attempt at remote control of course. But I'm glad that several years later, I was able to spend more time with my sister during the spring when she needed me most. We split and stacked several cords of firewood together, visited Greg in the hospital and I thanked her friends for being so kind and helpful.

With each trip we take, I realize we experience mild to moderate culture shock. Some would call it adjustment, that slightly sinister psychological term for adapting to new conditions and, as with B movies, being assessed by others as to the success of the transplant or brainwashing or whatever. I've experienced culture shock and I've helped other people understand what it is they are going through. After spending months living and working in tents and huts in India and Sri Lanka, sleeping on a bamboo mat or a thin mattress that was home to two different kinds of bugs, or curled up on the floor of a train next to a bag of dried fish, eye to eye with a deceased cod, I'd stood in a Montreal department store before a display of deodorants, laughing non-stop. My friend had to gently lead me out of the place to avoid a scene. The absurdity of one world juxtaposed with another simply overcame me. All I had done for months on end was sweat buckets hoeing fields of chilies and onions, building roads by hand with work gangs, or, most memorably, singing folk songs with fellow Crossroaders Margot Vanderham and Allan Archibald before several hundred Tamil teachers in 39C heat.

Some people get angry and paranoid with their overseas hosts for not being North American enough, despite being taught beforehand to grasp some fundamental cultural differences, but that's at an intellectual level. Culture shock is about perception and emotions, righteous fixed beliefs or tolerance, maintaining a sense of identity, a sense of humour and feeling safe—or not. It can be tricky. Sometimes people do just want your money or your belongings or, having had to work with a few ethically challenged people myself, sometimes it has very little to do with cultural differences and everything to do with an inflated sense of personal entitlement coupled with a complete lack of self-awareness or character. Immersed in another culture, we become the Other: a foreigner in the minority for perhaps the first time in our lives, retreating to our books or blocking out the world with music via earbuds, or adopting a sudden interest in solitary meditation. Or talking obsessively to anyone who will listen about All Things Perfect Back Home, fearful of the new, overwhelming environment. Now I observe myself going through a similar sort of experience, a mild but definite transition similar to culture shock, every time I come off the lightstation.

Like Molly Brown when she first saw and heard vehicles hurtling by at fifty kilometres an hour as we walked on a residential city sidewalk, I jump out of my skin, twirl around and tangle my leash around the nearest pair of legs. No, wait, that's her, not me. What I do is stare at the new cars, at people, store windows, billboards, buildings under construction, everything. I look people right in the eye until I realize that makes a lot of strangers uncomfortable and then I quickly remind myself to dial it down, to settle into the casual, eyes-averted, diffident ways of the Western world. Going from a tiny island, population two or three, to any kind of human settlement brings out my own brand of personal intensity, but also my avid and ongoing curiosity about new things in the wider world.

I hear myself chatting away to store clerks and post office workers and I tell myself, "Just slow down! You're sounding like a Yukon trapper again, that guy who hasn't seen another human being for six long, dark weeks of winter! Just shut up or they'll think you're as crazy as an outhouse rat!" I apologized for talking so much to one writer friend and she just smiled and reassured me that I'm always interesting. Days later it occurred to me that she might mean I am an interesting specimen, as in a character study serving as a warning to others, not that my rapid-fire commentary about all and sundry topics was terribly fascinating. Oh dear.

I also find myself increasingly impatient with pompous, unhelpful or rude people of all ages. I have to struggle mightily to curb my tongue. I'm just not exposed to nearly as many annoying people that I'm forced to be nice to anymore. I'm out of practice with social niceties, I guess. So when someone is nasty to me, say via the internet, where the trolls now lurk under the world's biggest bridge, or in person, maybe because they are enacting their own version of a power trip, I long to tell the familiar or the faceless cowards exactly what I think of them. But I usually manage to ignore idiots, politely set the oblivious straight and then avoid them all as much as possible, which tempered restraint civilization depends upon. Plus, it's always wise to avoid a battle of wits with an unarmed jerk.

This is when I know that spending so much time by myself can lead to me being a cranky old beast who suffers fools and fatheads not at all gladly. I do not wish to join the Tinfoil Hat Brigade of cabin and condo dwellers who spend their days online spewing diatribes at each other. Wasn't I aiming for a serene wise woman persona by the time I was a revered elder? Whenever that is, possibly ninety in my case. I'm still too full of piss and vinegar to float around with a detached attitude to worldly strife or to let the people temporarily in charge of provincial and federal governments wreck my country, including a destructive and expensive boondoggle like the Site C Dam on the Peace River, without a peep. My all-time hero is Marg, "Princess Warrior"! But then again I also don't want to become one of those lightkeepers who thinks the Outside World is a sinful place with a bunch of sinning sinners all going straight to Hell in a shiny red handcart.

We love going on adventures and now that we can take actual holidays, interspersed with family visits, we make the most of them. Jeff is good at surfing the net to research the possibilities and so far, we've booked a month in a private beach villa with a dip pool on the Yucatán peninsula. There I finished the second-to-last draft of *The Village of Many Hats*, writing almost every morning and reading and swimming in the afternoon. We booked a month-long Amtrak rail pass with a sleeping compartment, a fantastic deal, which took us from Seattle to San Francisco, Chicago, New Orleans and San Antonio on a blues, BBQ and film festival extravaganza that might possibly be our best holiday ever.

Near San Antonio, we stayed with writer and long-time friend Paulette Jiles, who had visited us on Lennard Island in 2009 when she was researching and writing her novel *Lighthouse Island*. When Jeff sent her his annual photography wall calendar, she forwarded an image of our lighthouse on a foggy night to her editor at HarperCollins in New York. She liked it too and most crucially, so did the art department. Voila, Jeff's photo graced the covers of Paulette's brilliant novel in the USA, Canada and the UK.

Looking ahead, we want to take longer holidays to Europe and to Southeast

Caroline, Paulette Jiles (far right), Seamus and his girlfriend, Georgina Lorimer. Caroline and Jeff first met Paulette when she was teaching at David Thompson University Centre in 1983. This was a personal visit but also allowed Paulette to do some research for her novel *Lighthouse Island*.

Asia, to visit family and friends there and to see new sights. It's all a balance of work, family, saving for retirement and writing as we head toward the home stretch, the last third of our lives together. But I won't retire from writing until I pop my clogs. Fall off my twig. Keel over in my gumboots. Some day my ship will come in. As Jack Kerouac said, "Genius gives birth, talent delivers." I tell myself that good writers, like good guitar players, are a dime a dozen and that only those of us who work really, really hard and who stretch our repertoire and work well with others will deliver. Which is to say that not everyone who sings in their morning shower should expect to debut at Carnegie Hall. As with culture shock, it's tricky, and the fear of self-delusion lurks like a vulture with bad breath near the desk of every honest writer I know, snickering and whispering something that sounds a lot like *fraud, fool, ho-hum, boo-hoo, keep your day job*.

There is also, as with my Montreal deodorant debacle, the return to so-called normal, a reverse culture shock if you will. We must eventually come home to our rocky green island, strap on the harness, do the shift work, embrace the solitude as well as the sociable dinners at the picnic table with the million-dollar ocean view, all of it. Homeward bound, for now, our roaming done for another year, our power shop at Costco and browsing at Value Village for work clothes done, our teeth to our toes all inspected by medical and dental professionals and declared good to go, we are ready to come home. We start by boarding a helicopter at the base in Victoria and if we're lucky, the coast is clear and we start flying north, hoping for a southeast tailwind to bring us home in just over an hour.

Sometimes we are tasked by the Coast Guard to check out a report of wreckage and so we circle down to stare at the chunks of a fishing boat, with netting and floats still attached to the stern, but no name or identifying numbers in sight. The pilot's index finger taps in the GPS coordinates for the wreckage. Or we touch down on a remote beach to identify a washed-up buoy, half a ton or more of sea-battered metal. Jeff always has his camera handy so he sprints out to photograph it and will email the shots back to the Coast Guard people who deal with stranded buoys. We look down at the waterfalls of the West Coast Trail and the waving, trudging hikers, the big swells and the hollowed caves. We scoot under the fog if we have to and at other times zoom through it to get above it.

Other days we hang on grimly, keeping quiet while the pilot handles the chopper being battered by strong gusting winds or thermal updrafts that feel like the hand of a mean giant child playing with us. One day the pilot and I, the only passenger, were tasked with assisting a ground search for a missing man. We were asked by Search and Rescue to cover a specific area of shoreline and sea while ground search parties looked elsewhere. We flew back and forth over the assigned territory four times, each of us peering down into the heavily forested land, the area near the river overflowing its banks and brown with the silt and debris of spring runoff, and the sullen green-grey ocean. We saw the black roof of the vehicle the man left behind and we heard radio talk about his dog found running free, the first tip-off that all was not as it should be.

The pilot and I both had the same feeling, which he quietly expressed: "I

Photo taken inside the Bell 212 en route to a relief assignment. The gear goes behind the pilot and engineer, and Jeff and Caroline sit in the back.

don't think this search will end well." I agreed. We both heaved heavy sighs. And it didn't end well. But there are more happy endings out here than sad ones, like the hikers whose shortcut across the bog got them thoroughly lost with nightfall approaching and who were spotted by our airborne pilot and engineer, who then radioed the ground search crew with the exact GPS location.

But we human beings always remember the ones we couldn't find and couldn't save, the child swept off the rocks, the young man in the sinking boat in the dark, the passengers and the pilot on the float plane, the dying whale gouged by a boat propeller or strangling slowly in a fishnet. We are haunted by radio voices, by fragments of a boat washed up or airplane wreckage below us—or even worse, never finding a single piece of evidence of people who just disappeared forever from their families.

For many lightkeepers, the pilots are the people with whom we have the most open and frank discussions about our lives and working conditions, and we certainly feel bonded to them when we survive a particularly stressful flight together. Most of them have a sense of humour, which surely must be a job requirement for dealing with bureaucracy and isolated lightkeepers in various mental states, desperate to get out for whatever reason. They might even meet hugely relieved keepers, holiday-bound at last for Cuba or Costa Rica or Croatia, as long as they can get to the airport on time later that same day, after being stormbound on their station two days in a row. The giddy joy of making that holiday flight elevates us all in the southbound chopper.

Sometimes there is no helicopter available due to mechanical issues or the weather is just plain awful. We are then booked onto the Tofino Lifeboat Station's Zodiac, which can usually handle our tricky Lennard Island channel and the ramp, where, if we are tall and nimble and the tide comes to mid-ramp, we spring on board like gazelles wearing lifejackets. Or, if the tide is low, and the lifeboat hovers above our short selves, we make brave and desperate leaps up at the looming rubberized prow between giant surges of water, assisted by one or two crew members above with vigorous yanks on both arms and Jeff shoving my orange floater suit in the general area of my rear end to heave me up and on board. (Jeff more recently built me a clever set of mini-stairs out of wood so I can now make a more dignified entrance, most of the time.) The flotation suit, size medium, is still far too long in the leg for me, so I have to cinch the thing up around my boots, knees and waist. I feel like the Pillsbury Dough Person in orange, constrained by several tight bands at crucial spots. I can hardly bend my knees let alone spring up like a pursued gnu onto a boat one or more metres higher than myself.

After I hop (or flop) up into the big Zodiac, I sit in the saddle, keeping my knees as soft as I would when riding a loping horse that might make sudden jumps in turbulent water, an airborne plummet downwards or a furtive sideways leap alongside a rolling two-metre swell. There are good handles to grip with both hands as well. Suddenly the constrictions of the flotation suit are replaced by its true warmth and protection from the piercing wind and cold salt water, except what ends up splashed over my exposed face. It's a thrill ride for me, every single time.

Getting off the lifeboat is much easier, a mighty leap between surges onto our ramp, with dogs and other personnel standing out of the way and well back, preferably. But an unexpected surge of water swivelling the prow sideways at the last second can mean that a solid landing on the ramp is transformed into one foot on the ramp and the other plummeting down into the ocean. Ditto getting my wretched gumboot trapped in the tight space at the very pointy end of the prow. We have all been baptized at the ramp: mildly, as with filled gumboots, moderately, with wet clothing up to the waist, or the full immersion ceremony. We have all survived.

What I do know for sure is that I am always glad to go away, to see my friends and family again and to travel to new countries or return to favourite cities, like Seattle, for live music and other creative inspiration. Jeff and I both love art galleries and live concerts and movies on big screens, and we especially love being back in real bookstores. We go to restaurants and order things we've never had before and we enjoy every minute of being out in the cities of this world, getting our urban buzz, thanks to the life and people only cities can offer.

I always love coming home too, from the initial running around to see which flowers are blooming, to a more thorough examination of how the gardens are surviving or even thriving. I love our own coffee and our own food again, sated with the seafood of New Orleans and Texas BBQ or delicious Mayan breakfasts. I need to retreat from the hubbub of travel and a social life just to clarify, contemplate and unravel all the possibilities for writing.

I sort through the genres to match my content. Play or poem? Short story or novel? Children's novella or a long poem, possibly a picture book? A saleable and timely magazine or newspaper piece, perhaps? Until the lighthouse life, I rarely stopped my hectic pace of living long enough to write about what I was actually up to in the moment except for in my journal. Besides, I never felt that I knew enough or had the right amount of perspective to write about my own life. I preferred to sort things out with fiction, which was more fun, as well as an easier way to tell the truth.

Before finding this perfect environment for writing, I'd usually trade my time and services to find ways to retreat and a space in which to write. Off I'd go to take care of a friend's condo, with an aquarium or incontinent elderly dog to maintain, or to look after a small farm and its chickens, ducks, geese and troika of vociferous dogs. I began my early short stories for *Disturbing*

Caroline, while on a book promotion tour for her novella *The Village of Many Hats*, finds promotional material on BC Ferries. *Photo by unknown tourist*

the Peace in a Yalakom Valley summer cabin, a former first aid skid shack sans electricity, and then moved into a log cabin once used by cowboys on trail drives. I looked after a Houdini hound posing as a purebred pooch and a million-dollar West Coast cedar and glass edifice in the Gulf Islands. I lived in a tent and wrote on park picnic tables. I lived in my Dodge Tradesman 100 van. One October I spent a rare month in a studio in Banff's Leighton Artists' Colony, writing most of *Alaska Highway Two-Step* in a studio inside a refurbished 1948 fishing boat. Another October I lived in a simple monastery room in St. Peter's Abbey in Muenster, Saskatchewan, a place where I wrote like a spring unsprung, singing vespers with the monks at 5:15 every afternoon. There I completed five short stories for my literacy book contract and wrote another story about a nun with a secret life, which after three years and many drafts found its way into ROOM, another little and long-lived Canadian literary magazine. It will also find a place in my next collection of short fiction. But don't hold your breath. I write like a glacier, compressing and releasing rare and ancient layers of water ever so slowly. Although in this era, glaciers are moving and melting at an unprecedented rate. Likewise, I must pick up the pace.

I have done my best writing in these places, with sociable time scheduled amidst the solitude, surrounded by the purity of wide open spaces or the mountains. I can only put my best efforts into being an extrovert for so long. I will eventually burn out unless I can get to a quiet place to think and create, to write and inhabit my own worlds. And I've always been this way. Half-extrovert, half-introvert, one half of me leaping gleefully up challenging rapids with my fin-folk leaping all around me, the other half silent and still, lurking in a deep pool away from all the noise and chaos.

Now I have my own retreat and Time—wonderful unspooling days and months in which to think and read and write. I have a room, almost, of my very own, a room with an ocean view past the mountain ash tree. Virginia Woolf would approve.

SIXTEEN

First Storm Choka

Storm warning alert
bring it on, we yell, full force
northwest fifty knots
our hatches are battened
down, our heads bowed
we lean against our doors
grin, try to ignore the roar

A Day, a Week, a
Month on the Job

THE NEW YEAR HAS BEGUN AND I'M BACK TO WORK AS THE ASSISTANT lightkeeper on Lennard again. After looking at the to-do list in the radio room office, I've picked my task. I will trim and nail down roofing shingles on our winch house stairs and on the observation deck next to the radio building. They will prevent us from slipping and falling and possibly breaking parts of ourselves in the bargain. A relatively cheap solution, it's the kind of job I especially like to do when the January sun peeps out from the Great Grey Sky and there is even an encouraging hint of warmth in it. The winch house stairs are sheltered by several big spruce trees and a dense salal hedge. I reuse as many of the old flat-headed shingle nails as possible, using the claw hammer to pry them up carefully so as not to crush their thin galvanized heads.

I am transported to my childhood and my sister and I helping Dad by straightening old nails while he builds a granary. Our fingers suffer more mashing than the nails ever do but we learn the necessary fine motor skills eventually and the confidence to swing a hammer.

As I finish the second row of shingle footprints to the observation deck on the shady side of the building, I whack in the nails with three good swings, rarely needing four, and finish the job before the showers of icy rain advance from the ocean and drench the island.

Since the beginning of January, we've had high winds, cold, frosty nights (glad am I that I pruned the rose bush already), and lots and lots of drizzle and fog. Drizzle so fine I call it West Coast face lotion. My face feels spritzed by a gentle Nordic goddess or one of her pantheon of spa attendants as I sprint up the stairs to do my weather observations.

It was also a week when both of us were in the grip of purging and cleaning out old clutter of all kinds: paper, as in ancient income tax envelopes, books we no longer needed to lug around with us, clothing that has sat in my mending pile, waiting to be hemmed and fixed with my snazzy Swiss sewing machine, for years. There is emotional baggage and then there is just plain junk. I certainly don't ever want to move with a pile of unsorted papers taking up cargo room, and while I have to be in a certain ruthless if not bloody-minded mood to summon the energy to go after my own detritus, I feel mentally and physically lighter for having done so.

I am amazed at how much I have winnowed the wheat from the chaff— and some wild oats that I do not want bruited about when I'm mouldering in the grave and cannot so much as shake a bony fist. All incriminating juvenilia ends up in the cleansing flames of our station incinerator.

It is such a liberating feeling, to label and pack away rejection (lots) and acceptance (fewer but more highly prized) letters and certificates and book reviews, knowing I will never use them again and therefore, the burden of carrying them around from place to place is *poof!* gone, or at least sensibly reduced. I organized the piles of paper into their eras by date and activity: education, theatre, political activism, BC Arts Council, Selkirk College and Vancouver Foundation boards and committees, ditto Caravan Stage Theatre, Theatre Energy, the David Thompson University Library 96-Day Occupation, Kootenay School of Writing, Slocan Lake Gallery Society, all done and dusted.

Writing, always writing throughout, from the first poem published in Lanark County's *Soya Grit*, circa 1978, and all my *Alaska Highway News* columns and articles in the late sixties, to innumerable unpublished drafts of short stories and long poems, eight years' worth, which eventually found homes in Canadian literary magazines and finally in *Disturbing the Peace*, all tucked away into their own manila envelopes. I carefully removed my tear sheets from five years' worth of *Kootenay Review* magazines, artist profiles and book reviews with a few lighthearted travel pieces about my National Book Week Festival tour of North and South Peace River libraries in 1990 featuring a photo myself waving, in front of the tiny Pouce Coupe Municipal

Library. There is another favourite, courtesy of a Sunshine Coast Festival of the Written Arts appearance in 1992, with Peter Gzowski, Sylvia Dorling and myself waving from a sleek convertible (Peter needed cigarettes and my friend—and erstwhile paparazzo—Barbara Cruikshank also had the snazzy wheels). I rediscover my Aunty Verbosity cartoons, a persnickety old gal in a rocking chair knitting entire scarves of social commentary. I wish I'd done more of them. I remind myself it is never too late to leap onto a new career path. Oh well, I console myself, so many ideas, so little time left to execute them all. I keep the dozen or so pages of cartoons, unable to toss them and justifying it because they take up so little room... but with regret, I toss postcards from people whose first names are all I have—for the life of me, I cannot recognize their handwriting or place them in any context. I cannot change or dwell on the past and with this lighthouse work, it's best to stay securely in the present.

Earlier in the week, Jeff and I tackled another grubby job, the changing of the oil in the duty engine. It is hot, noisy, smelly work at the best of times, but the engine had run its four thousand hours. We had to switch over to the "A" engine, a bigger, noisier brute than the "B," which is our regular duty engine. The "A" should run for twenty-four hours at least once a month, just to keep it ready for emergencies when it will automatically kick in and take over from the failing duty engine. This happens when there is an overload in usage, something as simple as having two clothes dryers and an oven on in separate residences, for example. When all three houses are in use, all of us usually remember to check with the others before using the dryer especially, a real energy hog. We do have clotheslines as well, and we make use of them whenever weather permits.

We brought a waste oil barrel into the engine room and set up the portable pump motor with two hoses attached to it nearby. One hose was shoved down into the empty barrel while the other was placed inside the sump of the engine to slurp up the used, hot, black oil. The pump also had a cord that plugged into an electrical outlet. Once the waste oil was flowing from the engine's sump down into the waste oil barrel, Jeff motioned me outside to talk where we wouldn't need ear protectors.

Right then I experienced one of my psychic moments and was very uncomfortable about it because, of course, it is not a rational thing to envision oil gushing everywhere. But it was so strong a feeling that after Jeff said something about the oil change process, what we had to do next or something normal like that, I said, "We've gotta get back inside." As I opened the door, I saw the hose that had been inside the waste oil barrel come writhing up out of the barrel like a python in reverse to begin spraying black oil everywhere.

I stood there, stunned at the sight of the demonic hose gushing oil, seeing what I had just "seen" actually happening. Jeff, bless him, took one look at my shocked face and then at what I was staring at and jumped for it, picking up the hose and jamming it back down into the barrel. The pulsing peristalsis of the electric pump had created enough momentum to move a metre of hose up and out of the receptacle. It had never happened before, Jeff told me later. There was a fair amount of spent oil on the floor, on the engine itself and on us too, but we used the industrial cleaner of choice on lightstations, a.k.a. The People's Friend, Dustbane full-strength. We used piles of absorbent fuel spill sheets and cleaning cloths so that within the hour, while we refilled the engine with clean oil, we completely finished the messy job.

That week we were also pleasantly surprised by a visit from the four crew members on shift at the Tofino Lifeboat Station. One of the gang had worked at the station for more than fifteen years but had never actually set foot on Lennard Island. He'd been in a wetsuit and swum through the narrow surge channel between Lennard and Lesser Lennard, though, a watery adventure not for the unskilled or faint-hearted. We took them on the Grand Tour of the radio building attic, a treasure trove of supplies, with twelve dustpans, another dozen toilet scrubbers, at least ten axe handles, old Swedish-style timber saws and many other hoarded oddities. There once was a box of plain white cans proudly labelled "The Cleaner of the 80s!" but someone cleaned up and the much-touted box became a casualty to a tidy mind. Then, before trudging up all sixty-seven steps of the tower for photo opportunities, we toured them through our radio room, workshop, the gym in the old engine room and the foghorn room, with its two massive galvanized steel tanks that look like something out of a steampunk film. The foghorn's compressor was removed in 2003, a casualty of budget cuts... local boaters still miss it.

Once I was off-duty over at Beaches Plaza getting my hair bucked off in the stylish Aveda salon, as were two other local women. One bed and breakfast owner (cut and blonde streaks) told me she used to tell guests who were complaining about the noise of the Lennard foghorn that it was just the whales mating. A most unladylike eruption of guffaws erupted from all three chairs and the attending stylists at the thought of the city slickers dining out on this hokum forevermore.

For dinner that evening, I chopped one bunch of fresh garden celery, courtesy of surplus baby celery plants that Patti, my gardening buddy at Cape Beale Lightstation, sent up to us last spring, then sacrificed three baby leeks and several large kale leaves for our beef pot pie. I cursed the young two-point buck deer that swam over to Lennard from Wickaninnish or Echachis Island to eat my edamame soybeans and winter cauliflower and purple sprouting broccoli and most of the kale as well. I started each of these plants from one tiny seed back in July and nurtured them through two separate transplantings to get them to flourish in the winter garden beds. If Mister Young Buck isn't a goner (he definitely left Lennard before Christmas and I suspect Molly chased him off the island back into the sea), he'll remember the tasty unprotected garden beds and return with his extended family in tow. But I will tip off certain biped friends with firearms for a share of the cloven-hoofed beast should he set his pointy toes down here again.

As befits January and February, we are being battered by high winds and rain, rain, rain. The eagles are in their element, coasting on the gusts, their big wings spread out and trembling slightly, adjusting to the speed and direction of the winds in a superb Big Top act hovering above us. Then they swerve and dive through the spruce grove on our island, back and forth, up and down, the pair of them engaged in an obstacle course race. The smaller birds have found a protected spot somewhere out of sight to wait out the winter storms, but the eagles are having a heyday in this barrage. Their high chittering calls and dares and double-dare exploits delight us, the earthbound, below them.

The rhythms of steady relief work on our home station in mid-winter allow me to write nearly every morning, guilt-free, and to start my shift at noon and deliver my first weather report by 1240 hours. I need to check the engine room gauges, wipe down the duty engine, clean any oil spatter on the floor, eyeball the gauges on the tanks and confirm which tank is supplying the fuel to make sure its levers are pointing in the right direction, so as not to starve the day tank inside the engine room of fuel, and do a walk-around inspection to make sure there are no signs of leakage from the tanks or the fuel line.

The stormy sogginess of our winters means that the endless maintenance of our eleven buildings and our grounds has pretty much ceased. Unless a chunk of metal roof blows off or a basement floods, both of which we've experienced and fixed, we can settle down to our woodworking and other projects with the hatches battened and the tea kettle on. All the lawn mowers and hand clippers, all the wooden handles of the rakes and shovels need inspection, cleaning and sharpening, and some need oiling too. It is pleasant work, "puttering" as Dad would call it, going from one relatively minor but necessary task to another.

Jeff has become, as one Coast Guard colleague described him, MacGyver Jeff. He's made all sorts of driftwood side tables, coffee tables, coat hangers and towel racks. He's learned to install a new toilet (O Happy Day) and replaced a burned-out washing machine part so that the washer works just fine again. Instead of having a work crew come in at great expense with a little Kubota, he hand-dug a trench and used clay tile to build an effective drainage system around a chronically flooded crew house. He can troubleshoot asthmatic furnaces, too. He's also made countless trellises and protective chicken wire cages and Fred, the Cross-Dressing Scarecrow, for the garden. Bonus, he makes me laugh nearly every day as well.

This is not to say that Jeff and I never want to launch the Offending Other into the ocean some days but happily, these are relatively rare moments of strife, as we get wiser about battles and wars and which are worth fighting. We flare up, have our say, hear the other out and then it's over. We have the long view, and we're looking in the same direction at the same time.

And what of my list of personal improvement to-do's, penned back in August of 2008? I reread the list from time to time, heave a great sigh at some of the futile, if well-intentioned, goals and try to cut myself a bit of slack as well. Life is not a foot race. It's more like a grand obstacle course with stops for picnics along the way.

1. LEARN TO PLAY A MUSICAL INSTRUMENT. I can't sing in choirs anymore, which feels odd after singing in so many, in so many places. I guess I'll be a musician in my next life. I am a writer now.

2. LEARN SPANISH. We have phrase books, CDs and a proper language lesson kit, all inspired by our first holiday to Cuba in 2009 where we were limited by our lack of fluency. Baby Spanish. The CDs are waiting until I finish writing the final draft of this book, however, as I cannot focus on any other language. Once again, it's all about writing being the number one priority right now.

3. BECOME VERY FIT AND HEALTHY. Despite being dealt the genetic black spot for osteoarthritis in my knees, I have been actively compensating for years of sedentary work. Our station has dozens of stairs leading from each dwelling to the land bridge and down to the boat ramp. I am kayaking with confidence on two-metre-plus ocean swells and I have yet to flip, although my surf landings often lack finesse and dignity. What matters most is fitness, both mental and physical, plus a sense of humour and an optimistic attitude. I'm well on my way thanks to our gym and healthy diet but, like the report card comments section says: Room For Improvement.

4. BECOME A REALLY GOOD BREAD BAKER. This makes #3 harder to achieve but I do have a passion for making good food. If, years from now, you see a raucous old lady pushing a walker with a basket filled with loaves of artisan breads, peddling them on the street, that'll be me, augmenting my old age pension. In between sending poems to literary magazines for the really big bucks, of course.

5. WRITE, WRITE, WRITE. I now aim to write two books a year and to start at least four, plus forty good poems. This includes children's picture books, novellas for teens and pre-teens, as well as books for adults. I am also steadily amassing short stories for my next collection, pulling together a first collection of poetry and,

God help me, tackling another adult novel. Now is my time to write, I know it and I won't blow it.

6. REDISCOVER LONG-BURIED FLAIR FOR VISUAL ARTS BY QUILTING AND PAINTING AGAIN. This has been a humbling experience. After spending hundreds of dollars on gorgeous fabrics, a sewing machine and quilting supplies, I attempted oven mitts, my first quilting project since a night school class in 1977 when I made a cathedral window cushion using my handmade batik cloth, all painstaking handwork. It is still lovely. My oven mitt result? Eight layers of material meant for a ham-handed giant with freakishly short thumbs. I struggled with the tension on my brand new sewing machine. I struggled with what I imagined I could do with the beautiful fabrics and the reality, which is that it's been decades since I've made anything more complex than Christmas gift bags or mended jeans or sewn some simple yet memorable Halloween costumes for Seamus. Art, no matter what the form, is always a blank page. The artist is always a beginner. Patience is a virtue and all that crap. I am a writer not a quilter.

7. LEARN TO LOVE SOLITUDE. LEARN TO ACCEPT AND LOVE MYSELF, FLAWS, VIRTUES, THE WHOLE EMPANADA. This is always harder than it seems or sounds. The solitude part has been easier than I first imagined. After all my years filled with long to-do lists and piles of paper, the uncluttered life on an island with three humans and two dogs, and for a while, our old Woodycat, may he rest in peace on Lennard Island forever, is balm to my overheated brain. I never tire of looking at the ocean. I have learned to be mostly accepting of rain. It's just something to measure and report in our line of work. I love the sunny days, don't get me wrong, but I love the thunderous storms and surging seas just as much. As for the second half of the equation, it's a work in progress. I'm harder on myself than anyone else could ever be—if only my inner critic would occasionally shut up.

"Make not your thoughts your prisons," Shakespeare advised. That is my real challenge out here.

8. EMBRACE LIVING IN ISOLATION AS A COUPLE AND MAKING A GOOD RELATIONSHIP EVEN BETTER. It's a risk to expose any relationship to such intense solitude and more than a few have confided that they could not do what we are doing as a couple. Frankly, we're both first-born from families of four siblings. We both come from small rural communities. We're very similar in so many ways. We have rousing, infrequent fights because we're both always right, of course, but we've been loving partners, best friends and each other's first readers and editors since 1986. We count our blessings to have found each other and hope to die within minutes of each other. It doesn't get much better and we both know it.

9. LEARN TO LOVE AND APPRECIATE EVERYTHING ABOUT THIS LIFE. Gratitude is the heart of prayer, my dear friend Evelyn once told me. Practise daily. So if anyone sees me lifting both arms high in the air and hears something like a song with simple lyrics sounding like "Thank you, Big Wild Universe, thank you," well, yeah, that'll be me, overcome with gratitude, my heart pumping with joy. I am the happiest I've ever been.

10. BECOME CONTENT. AGE GRACEFULLY.

Wisdom arrives when it does and better it arrives late than never. And it's easier to pick up on with the noise and clutter stripped away, with only the rhythmic wash of the waves and the wind pushing through the spruce trees. Here there is time to think, to marvel, to let go of grudges and regrets, to solve real and imaginary problems, to write day after day, to be content with what I have, where I am and who I am. Until Life throws a curve ball, and then I will cope, as I have always coped, and I will adapt to the necessary changes. But I must not judge myself harshly if I am not successful in this day and age. Therefore, to write is enough. To amuse, inform or entertain, to make you, dear Reader, laugh and cry, is the icing on the cake. As for aging gracefully, well, some days I'm considerably more graceful than others and

I'm more preoccupied with treating aches and pains effectively than in the previous decades... fortunately so are my dearest friends so we swap ailment stories via email and during visits, apologizing intermittently for sounding like tiresome old geezers. Another friend reminds me that the Chinese expression for long-time friends, the ones who knew us when we were all nimble and lithe, is "Same-Olds," which is perfect. Once we get together for a visit, the decades drop away and we are all in grade nine again, just older and wiser and more secure and kinder. We all still laugh the same and that is the clincher. I cherish my old friends.

Sometimes, though, I need to escape the island just to see other people, like my lovely friends on Vargas Island or my bookseller and writer friends in Tofino, who understand that just to yak about the books we're writing or reading, and kids and pets and gardens, is a sociable mental health break for me. I usually fumble some appropriate social filters into place so that I don't blurt non-stop like that garrulous Yukon trapper. Sometimes I've been able to head off to perform at festivals with my Clayoquot Writers Group gang or to fly solo at other literary events, and to work with children in schools and libraries all over BC and as far south as Utopia, Texas. It takes a lot of preparation time and energy to create props and different presentations and to drive from one place to the next. But there is nothing better than meeting a beaming nine-year-old who loves my book because one of the characters, Mrs. Singh, makes samosas and pakoras. The beautiful little girl in grade three from Maple Ridge had never read about the delicious food her own mother makes in a school book ever before. I love presenting my own books to children and showing them how *Singing Away the Dark* looks in the French, Korean and Bulgarian editions.

What this lighthouse life means to me as a writer is that there are no more excuses for not writing. I am warm and dry and the roof overhead comes with Jeff's salary. I have looked ahead with unsentimental eyes and seen that I have at most thirty years of living left, if the Fates are kind and I've inherited the long-life genes of the women on both sides of my family tree. What interferes most with my writing time, though, is the addiction of email. Solution: shut down the internet connection during writing time. The other sad fact is that I no longer have the energy or stamina to write much during the evenings, as I did during my single, TV-free decades. Now I love to spend my evenings wrapped in a blanket in the armchair watching detective mysteries... It's so very easy to escape the hard solitary work of writing.

This is why God invented deadlines. This is why my dear, departed friend Lorna Obermayr, artist and art professor emeritus, convenor of the Ladies Friday Salon in her New Denver studio (my writing office was upstairs), warned me that we had to produce art as much as possible when we were relatively young and strong and could stand, or sit, and focus for many hours on end, with fire in our brains and hearts and bellies, and with enough creative oomph to produce brilliant or at least audacious art.

It feels so very good to be writing steadily again and to be published instead of feeling like an irrelevant fool yodelling into the Abyss. Doing manual, repetitive work allows my mind to float around solving the literary problems I've created, whereas teaching creative writing or being a case worker for mentally challenged adults or bright and troubled teens eventually drains every ounce of smarts and excess energy I possess. Thus, my own writing dwindled, becoming a marginal part of my life. And who gets to live my Life? Why, only me, of course! I figured that out when I was fifteen but as with many life lessons, I've needed more than a few refresher courses.

This is so much better for me. It's not everyone's cup of tea but we each have to find the right environment in which to write our particular genres. I couldn't write plays out here in isolation, for example. Theatre needs collaboration with other people, workshopping the script-in-progress, hearing and seeing it up on its feet. Poetry, non-fiction essays, short and long fiction, children's literature, radio pieces or a memoir like this? All of these genres are possible, calling out for my attention, and if I run into a dead end in one project, I set that project aside for a while and pick up another genre to work and to play with, to keep the juicy life of the necessary, must-be-told stories flowing out through my fingertips. I write and rewrite until the piece hits the sweet spot. I swap work with several other writers online and I check in at the start of every month with my author friend Paula Wild to share trials and tribulations and to set our goals for the next month. We used to have Writer's Lunch once a month while I worked in the Comox Valley and we've continued the tradition online since I moved out to the lights. I've also taken an online course on writing a novel with editor, writer and UBC teacher Alison Acheson, which led to the novel I plan to rewrite next, the one set in 2060 in a watery world.

Fiction gives me the freedom to tell the truth by inventing 3-D characters and situations, even though I'm researching ocean currents and rates of glacial melt and the swirling mass of garbage in the Pacific Ocean. I want to travel the Northwest Passage for the sequel. I must take an oceanography course online.

Writing is never, ever boring to me. I tried to tell a seemingly bored grade nine Career Studies class this pertinent fact: it's so important to find work that truly interests us. One hand shot up and a belligerent young woman demanded to know whether my guest appearance and workshop would result in a mark. I had not been introduced by the teacher except to be told "They're all yours" before he headed out for a smoke or something, popping in and out of the class half a dozen times over the course of my visit. Here was a case in point, a teacher who clearly didn't want to be teaching and who was not willing to honour the school's Writing Festival guests either.

"Yes," I replied. "And your teacher will figure out how to do that."

Then I frogmarched them through most of my Great Canadian Literary Quiz, which totally flummoxed a few but also caused glinting eyeballs and little grins and thoughtful exhales during the rest of the hour, which fairly flew by. I left a mountain of pages on the teacher's desk and scooted off to catch a ferry for my next writing gig. Once again, a lesson in making the best of a semi-hostile predicament and consoling myself with the fact that my example and my efforts might positively influence at least one student in that class. Also, I had worked with another class earlier in the day led by a gifted, polite and professional teacher whose students clearly adored and respected her. In six days of Writing Festival work, her grade eleven/twelve English class was the most enthusiastic and, how shall I say this, Alive class I have had the pleasure of working with in many years. So it goes, the balancing act of Life, or to be more nautical about it, keeping an even keel in rough waters, aided by a spritely fair weather breeze.

Writing helps keep my brain cells agile—even if my knees creak.

SEVENTEEN

Mystery Flotsam Kouta

yearning, someone is, calling
I listen: silence
but there! far, so far at sea
log? totem? vanished…

Beyond These
Blue Horizons

O N OCCASIONS WHEN I'VE BEEN INTERVIEWED BY MEDIA ABOUT MY latest book, and this is humbling as well as frustrating, I find the reporter is often more interested in my lightkeeping work than my deathless contributions to Canadian literature. People want to know if I've saved lives (only my own, as far as I know) or done something dramatic and dangerous. Most of the truly gripping, life-saving incidents are accomplished by the Coast Guard lifeboat crews, who have several skookum boats at their dock and who are all trained and physically fit. Or the even more highly trained and super-fit Search and Rescue crews, who do things like dangle out of a helicopter to land on the deck of a ship where someone is injured or very ill. But lightkeepers have always done a lot of behind-the-scenes work to assist other Coast Guard personnel and the public.

In 2014, nine pleasure boaters from the BC mainland out on a day trip were rescued off Entrance Island when their power boat capsized. When the vigilant lightkeepers arrived in the relatively small but sturdy station boat, several of the people clinging to the hull were already suffering from hypothermia. Glenn Borgens and Jake Etzkorn saved them all. It was a proud moment for lightkeepers and vindicated the rationale that the public needs real, live lightkeepers keeping watch on the waters around their stations and well-maintained station boats at the ready. Despite the fact that some people, like one individual giving public presentations on BC Ferries, proclaim there are no lightkeepers actually working in BC and Newfoundland and Labrador (I set her straight by politely telling her and

Caroline is interviewed at Long Beach Radio's tiny studio in the ice house building on Tofino's waterfront. Geoff Johnson, to the left, was the host, and fellow guest, professional food lover Bobby Lax, the organizer of the Tofino-Ucluelet Culinary Guild, is to the right.

everyone in the room that there were fifty-seven lightkeepers in BC, including my husband), and others who, whatever their agenda might be, claim we don't contribute vital assistance and information to citizens, we do. In the summer of 2014, lighthouse keepers Toni Adams and Rena Patrick at Cape Beale heard yells in the dense fog and did a mayday relay that resulted in three people's lives being saved after their boat overturned in high seas. Likewise for Lynn Hauer and Wolfgang Luebke at Chatham Point in 2012, who heard a mayday at 3:00 a.m. and rescued two people and saved their sinking eighty-thousand-dollar boat by using the Honda pump stowed under the seat of their five-metre station boat.

Who would notice, as I did once while working at Estevan Point, that the light had gone dark? I roused the other keeper, fortunately Jeff, and we notified Coast Guard Radio to issue a warning on the continuous marine broadcast channel and then set about solving the electrical issue. We got the light turning and flashing again within twenty minutes of my noticing it on the way back to the house after my last evening weather report. A camera looking out to sea in a fixed location would not have noticed the light had stopped working. A lot of our work, including weather reports and routine problem-solving, prevents people from going out and getting into trouble, but of course nobody documents what doesn't happen. It doesn't make the six o'clock news unless it's high drama.

Who will stand guard to prevent wholesale looting and vandalism, the fate of many a de-staffed lightstation, or to call in a report of bunker oil oozing its way onto our beaches? Who will keep an eye out for enthusiasts on surfboards and paddleboards venturing far beyond their skill levels? Who will methodically document the temperature of the sea water so that scientists working with Fisheries have long-term data on hand? Who will have the observant eyes and helping hands to haul kayakers out of the water and to fill bathtubs with warm water to immerse their hypothermic bodies, as the keepers on Trial Island have done? Or to help hikers in shock after being stung by too many wasps or from having a camp stove blow up in their faces, or suffering a shattered leg like the keepers on the West Coast Trail and other wilderness trails have done for decades? Then there are the mystery boat sightings lightkeepers have called in, alerting authorities to drug smugglers, people smugglers and child abductions. Who will help when a fisherman has a heart attack and his buddy can't lift him out of the boat? And, in all these true situations, who would be there to use our equipment, our boats, stretchers, derrick, railway car, telephones and radios to call for appropriate help to assist with the rescue or the recovery of a body?

I remember a young First Nations man telling me he'd gone out with his friend when they were both twenty-one years old to fish and their GPS failed them. They kept Lennard Light in sight for many hours until they reached safe harbour. And I remember watching a sailboat make its way to safety into Friendly Cove at 2:30 a.m. after travelling all night in nasty weather. The next morning, I gave one young man, after learning this was his first sailboat experience ever, some blueberry muffins. His big smile was unforgettable. As was hearing a friend talk about being young and bringing a fishing boat up the west coast of the island in November, encountering such heavy swells off Pachena Point that he stayed out there talking to the lightkeeper all night until he felt calm and ready to tackle the homeward stretch.

Lightkeepers who love this life (and don't mind getting our gumboots filled with water from time to time) are a bargain early warning system, the lowest paid federal civil servants of all, and we are out here, already in place. In fact, we could do much more scientific data collection for any university or government department needing reliable, hardy year-round people on site. Certainly the scientists who install equipment to measure seismic activity wouldn't do so if those stations, like Carmanah and Nootka to name two that get thousands of visitors every summer, didn't have vigilant year-round lightkeepers. It's mundane work, but it's also valuable work and crucial work, all in the same day sometimes.

I admire my friends who are still doing Good Works and being useful in their communities, at the pinnacle of their careers. I am very proud of my accomplished and hard-working friends—don't get me wrong. But the litany of Things The World Needs Now makes me sigh deeply, sigh heavily and makes me recall endless work bees and even more endless meetings to organize the work bees. I have finally accepted that I will not save much of this world but I will also give myself a pat on the back for valiant effort over many years. I'm okay with that now. I've learned I cannot be all things to all people so I may as well be as true and kind and encouraging to the few I meet in this line of work, including myself, as I can.

We each have Time, Treasure or Talent to give our assorted good causes. Given my remote location, I no longer sit on boards and committees, but instead of time I donate my dribs and drabs of spare money to political and social causes, and I look forward to the helicopter bringing the provincial and federal electoral staff with the appropriate ballot box. The clerks all put their names in a hat as there is a long list of people who want to take the voting apparatus to our twenty-seven lightstations. To date, these are my jolliest voting experiences ever, even if the outcomes of late have made me fume uselessly after the fact.

I am not snooty about work and I will become the world's oldest waitress if I have to, albeit with a bionic knee and a large-print order pad. But until it comes to that, I have had some lovely letters from readers over the years affirming that my stories delight, comfort and are otherwise useful in all the right ways for other souls out there. I love my family and they love me and I am exceedingly rich in brilliant and inspiring friends all around the world.

So I have come to the conclusion that living on a green rock in the North Pacific Ocean is not a waste of my time and talents but rather the best possible way for me to be able to contribute my soul food to this world. Soup kitchen volunteering, and its social and political equivalent, must wait for when I live in the so-called real world again.

It's been a long apprenticeship becoming an author, and if I was to pinpoint the date of No Turning Back, it would be in April of 1981. I was in Nepal and my friend Pat and I went off to hike the trail to Muktinath in the Himalayas right after my work as a group leader in India was completed. Inspired by the lovely handmade rice paper I saw drying on easels facing the sun, I wrote a twelve-page story, *A Blue Fable*, and paid for it to be published on rice paper. I lugged 1,500 copies back to Canada. Then I learned about the nuts and bolts of selling and publicizing books from the ground up, literally. Bless the *Toronto Star* editor who had to fill newspaper space the day I called and who gave my adventure in Nepal a half-page with a massive photo (above the fold), thereby helping me sell hundreds of them in the city. Bless Beth Appeldoorn of Longhouse Books in Toronto who advised me to let the newspapers know about my book, and also showed me how to fill out an invoice properly.

Did I mention that writing pays poorly and it's getting worse, not better? It's the most difficult of all the jobs I've ever done to do really well, otherwise known as a satisfying yet frustrating paradox. As with farming, we writers are at the mercy of faraway market vagaries and mostly urban tastes, only with the weather playing less of a role for writers than farmers. Except me, perhaps? Anyway, I am now 99% okay with my remaining years being spent as a writer and writing about what matters to me. Just 1% of me would like to get rid of all this paper and clutter and forty years of letters and other sentimental crap I lug around, and to wear one cozy sort of robe, shave off this mop of hair, use one bowl and one spoon and sit at a desk with pencils and lots of blank paper.

Make that a laptop. With a reliable internet connection.

In my early adulthood I wasn't overly *mindful*, as Buddhist friends would observe, being instead the type who would sing for hours to combat boredom because it was distracting and fun just to sing with a hundred other people while building a road by hand, pausing only for our rice and vegetable curry lunch wrapped in banana leaves, or standing well back when the dynamite crew came in to blast out a nest of cobras. I was the type of person who more often chose to immerse herself in a new adventure and then later come up for air to reflect and to write about all I'd learned, rather than cautiously putting a toe in the water, mapping out my route and making observations about what everybody else was doing or thinking about doing.

I discovered I actually preferred leaping and then looking for an escape route if the pond was populated by crocodiles. I am a fast swimmer/learner, I can say truthfully, which doesn't mean that the total immersion method of living is pain-free and non-stop fun. Far from it. I have spent a fair amount of time on this earth reflecting at length on all the dumb mistakes—pardon me, opportunities for deeper learning—that ensued from my foolhardiness. But I

Three humpbacks surface close together off Nootka Island Lightstation.

have only a few lingering regrets and I am here today, typing this chapter in a warm, dry room in a Quatsino Lightstation house on Kains Island, population two adults, two dogs, five deer and a pair of bald eagles.

Finally, the bittersweet part. As soon as I came to live on the lights, I began to experience a kind of intense nostalgia for the present moment. I'd watch hungry Bohemian waxwings devouring still-green berries from the Sitka mountain ash tree outside my writing room window and feel a tug of sweet sorrow at my heart. Even more poignant was seeing and hearing a kingfisher mourning its mate for days after she had flown or been blown into a guy wire. We donated her body, frozen, to the Royal BC Museum in Victoria. Or in early spring at Nootka Light, to see Friendly Cove turn pale, milky green from dark grey-blue overnight, thanks to the herring spawn, and then to see all the birds and whales and other sea mammals gorging themselves on the delicious protein bonanza. We watched the Williams family harvesting roe from hemlock trees lowered into the water, as many as nine layers per branch. I served the raw herring roe soaked in tamari sauce on seaweed rice crackers to Ray Williams, who'd brought us a gift of several branches laden with roe, and to the electricians and the pilot working on the station that day as well.

I pinch myself. I am so lucky to witness this wilderness. I feel this urgency to remember, to memorize and to write the details down when I hear the gut-sick groans of the whistling buoy near Kains Island and walk the long boardwalk wending its way through the spruce and hemlock trees to the radio room. *Remember this sound, the pitiful bleats of the buoy keeping boats away from the rocks of Quatsino Sound, and the sea otter clapping prickly-shelled sea urchins to his chest.*

When we fly over the remote village of Kyuquot, I always think of my Aunt Vi Garrish Woodward, who worked as a Red Cross Outpost Hospital nurse there in 1940 when she was twenty-nine years old. I renew my vow to take the *Uchuck* tour and to walk where she once walked, to honour the aunt who gave me books. At 3:15 a.m., getting out to do my first weather report, when I hear the Chatham Point foghorn baritone *oooo-aaahhh* alternating with a cruise ship's booming bass horn as it heads from Discovery Passage into Johnstone Strait, and a fishing boat's assertive tenor toot coming in from

A sea otter does what sea otters do off Quatsino Lightstation.

Nodales Channel, all three of which converge below the station cliffs, I am thrilled. And then melancholy, thinking to myself: *Remember this, memorize the pitch and rise and fall of those sounds, because you will not hear them once you are far away from this life, this wonderful, amazing adventure.*

In Buddhism, *sankhara-dukkha* refers to the subtle sense of dissatisfaction with life because it is impermanent, because everything good will eventually change and, of course, end. The Gaelic word *dubhachas* is a melancholy term for that feeling of sadness during one of Life's Perfect Moments. The Japanese call it *mono no aware*, the sadness one experiences because beauty is fleeting. I've made a point of saying to the unsuspecting world daily that I am grateful to be alive, to hear this chittering eagle, to feel the delicate drizzle on my face, to find the first snowdrop blossoms in late January, to thank the so-called co-incidence of a runaway Jack Russell dog, which led to this opportunity, to live and work and write and love and learn as much as I can in the time I am given.

I count my blessings daily.

- *The End, So Far* -

Acknowledgements

THANK YOU TO EVERY KIND PERSON IN THE PAST FORTY YEARS WHO gave me a room—or cabin, cottage, condo or farmhouse—so that I could write. Thank you to all my teachers and all my students. Thank you to the editors and publishers at Canadian and American newspapers and magazines who published my stories, essays and poems and especially to all the editors and publishers of my books.

For crucial early support and encouragement, I am most grateful to Julian Ross, Maidie Hilmo, Allan Safarik, Betty Keller, Clark Blaise and Paulette Jiles. To all the librarians, booksellers, community arts council organizers and teachers who have made it possible for me to share my stories and to be paid, my most sincere thanks. I am so grateful to family, friends and fellow writers who stay in touch while I spend these years on splendid and remote lightstations. Our lively email and real mail exchanges have buoyed me over the Shoals of Despond and away from Dithering in the Garden to Avoid Writing. Your kind words and confidence in my efforts have nudged—or booted—me back to this desk time and time again.

Thanks also to Alan Twigg for encouraging me to write about my literary lighthouse life and for publishing the opening chapter which interested the best possible publisher for this project, the dynamite team at Harbour Publishing, including copyeditor Brianna Cerkiewicz and proofreader Cheryl Cohen, eagles in former lives, for whom even a nitpicker like myself is grateful when there are four possible spellings for one village. My thanks to book designer Shed Simas for his care and attention to the look of this book and being a pleasure to work with too. Likewise, my grateful thanks to publicist Annie Boyar for her creative energy while launching this book into the world. Anna Comfort O'Keeffe juggled all manner of sharp and dull objects with ease in her role as managing editor, while never once losing her sense of humour. My main editor, Pam Robertson, is as smart as a whip and tough as nails and she has saved me from myself in all the right ways for which I am eternally grateful! But she has to leave these clichés and that exclamation mark alone or I'll be forced to insert a smiley face.

Without Jeff George's sound advice, self-sacrifice and lifelong love of adventure—as well as the inspiration of his beautiful photography—this book would simply never have been written.

Suggestions for Your Own
Lighthouse Library

SOME TITLES ARE REFERENCE BOOKS OR HISTORY BOOKS, AND OTHERS are novels or poetry collections that resonate with this particular light-keeper. Then you too can play the parlour game to decide which ten books you'd take to a deserted island... and of those, which one book would you save? I still can't decide. But I do know that if I was allowed one song, it would be George Harrison's "Here Comes the Sun."

LIGHTHOUSE HISTORY

Guiding Lights: British Columbia's Lighthouses and Their Keepers, by Lynn Tanod, photographs by Chris Jaksa (Madeira Park, BC: Harbour Publishing, 1998).

Keepers of the Light: A History of British Columbia's Lighthouses and their Keepers by Donald Graham (Madeira Park, BC: Harbour Publishing, 1985).

Lighthouse Chronicles: Twenty Years on the B.C. Lights by Flo Anderson (Madeira Park, BC, Harbour Publishing, 1998).

The Lighthouse Stevensons by Bella Bathurst (London, UK: HarperCollins, 1999).

Lights of the Inside Passage: A History of British Columbia's Lighthouses and their Keepers by Donald Graham (Madeira Park, BC: Harbour Publishing, 1986).

We Keep a Light by Evelyn M. Richardson (Halifax, NS: Nimbus Publishing, 1945, 2005).

INDISPENSABLE REFERENCE BOOKS

Beyond the Outer Shores: The Untold Story of Ed Ricketts, the Pioneering Ecologist Who Inspired John Steinbeck and Joseph Campbell by Eric Enno Tamm (Vancouver, BC: Raincoast Books, 2004).

Bijaboji: North to Alaska by Oar by Betty Lowman Carey (Madeira Park, BC: Harbour Publishing, 2004).

Birds of North America: A Guide to Field Identification, expanded revised ed., by Chandler S. Robbins, Bertel Bruun and Herbert S. Zim (New York, NY: Golden Press, 1983).

The Book of Clouds by John A. Day (New York, NY: Sterling Publishing, 2006).

British Columbia: A Natural History, Revised and Updated by Richard and Sydney Cannings (Vancouver, BC: Greystone Books, 2004).

British Columbia Place Names, third edition, by G.P.V. and Helen B. Akrigg (Vancouver, BC: UBC Press, 1997)

The Cloudspotter's Guide by Gavin Pretor-Pinney (London, UK: Hodder and Stoughton, 2006).

The Cougar: Beautiful, Wild and Dangerous by Paula Wild (Madeira Park, BC: Douglas & McIntyre, 2013).

The Curve of Time by M. Wylie Blanchet (first edition: Edinburgh, Scotland: William Blackwood & Sons, 1961; 50th anniversary edition: Vancouver, BC: Whitecap Books, 2011).

Gardening When It Counts: Growing Food in Hard Times by Steve Solomon (Gabriola Island, BC: New Society Publishers, 2005).

An Intimate Look at the Night Sky by Chet Raymo (Vancouver, BC: Greystone Books, 2001).

The Last Great Sea: A Voyage through the Human and Natural History of the North Pacific Ocean by Terry Glavin (Vancouver, BC: Greystone Books, 2000).

The Last Island: A Naturalist's Sojourn on Triangle Island by Alison Watt (Madeira Park, BC: Harbour Publishing, 2002).

The Last Wild Wolves: Ghosts of the Great Bear Rainforest by Ian McAllister (Vancouver, BC: Greystone Books, 2007).

Lewis Clark's Field Guide to Wild Flowers of the Sea Coast in the Pacific Northwest by Lewis J. Clark (original edition: Sidney, BC: Gray's Publishing, 1974; later edition: Madeira Park, BC: Harbour Publishing, 2004).

Marine Life of the Pacific Northwest: A Photographic Encyclopedia of Invertebrates, Seaweeds and Selected Fishes by Andy Lamb and Bernard P. Hanby (Madeira Park, BC: Harbour Publishing, 2005).

National Audubon Society Field Guide to North American Weather by David Ludlum (New York, NY: Alfred A. Knopf, 1991).

The Nature of Shorebirds: Nomads of the Wetlands by Harry Thurston (Vancouver, BC: Greystone Books, 1996).

Pacific Reef & Shore: A Photo Guide to Northwest Marine Life by Rick M. Harbo (Madeira Park, BC: Harbour Publishing, 2003).

Plant Technology of First Peoples in British Columbia by Nancy J. Turner (Vancouver, BC: UBC Press, 1998).

Plants of Coastal British Columbia, including Washington, Oregon & Alaska, revised ed., compiled and edited by Jim Pojar and Andy MacKinnon (Vancouver, BC: Lone Pine Publishing, 1994).

Whales & Dolphins of the North American Pacific: Including Seals and Other Marine Mammals by Graeme Cresswell, Dylan Walker and Todd Pusser (Madeira Park, BC: Harbour Publishing, 2007).

White Slaves of Maquinna: John R. Jewitt's Narrative of Capture and Confinement at Nootka by John R. Jewitt (first published by John Jewitt in 1815, and many, many republications have followed; latest edition: Victoria, BC: Heritage House Publishing, 2010).

The Wolf Almanac by Jack H. Busch (New York, NY: Lyons & Burford, 1995).

A Year on the Garden Path: A 52-Week Organic Gardening Guide, revised second edition, by Carolyn Herriot (Madeira Park, BC: Harbour Publishing, 2011).

COOKBOOKS

Canadian Coast Guard 50th Anniversary Cookbook, Pacific Region,
compiled and edited by Linda Plamondon (Winnipeg, MB:
Rasmussen Company, 2012). Includes delicious contributions from
cooks and chefs in all four divisions of the Coast Guard, from
the ship's galleys of the fleet, the radio operators at MCTS, the
lightkeepers at BC lightstations and administrative staff at the bases
in Prince Rupert and Victoria.

Cooks Afloat! Gourmet Cooking on the Move by David Hoar and Noreen
Rudd (Madeira Park, BC: Harbour Publishing, 2001). A very useful
book with full-colour photographs. Includes vital information on
how to identify, catch and safely prepare tasty and healthy seafood
meals, in particular.

The Lighthouse Cookbook by Anita Stewart (Madeira Park, BC: Harbour
Publishing, 1988, 2001). Includes heirloom and inventive recipes
from BC lightkeepers in the late 1980s as well as lighthouse history
and pen and ink sketches of the existing lighthouses.

Malcolm Island Favourites: A Collection of Treasured Recipes Old & New
(Sointula, BC: Sointula Recreation Association, 2006). Highly
recommended for its treasure trove of authentic Finnish recipes and
many seafood recipes.

A HIGHLY RECOMMENDED LIST OF INSPIRING LITERARY WORKS
PERTAINING TO LIGHTHOUSES AND WATERY WILDERNESS AND WRITING

And See What Happens: The Journey Poems by Ursula Vaira (Halfmoon
Bay, BC: Caitlin Press, 2011). Wise and beautiful poems inspired
by three long journeys, including two marathon ocean-kayaking
voyages and one retreat to a wilderness cabin in the northern
Rockies. Deserves to become a BC classic.

Crowlogue, instigated by Adrienne Mason, writer, editor and publisher,
illustrated by Marion Syme (Tofino, BC: Postelsia Press, 2010).

Prose and poems by members of the Clayoquot Writers Group. An eloquent, many-voiced homage to the quintessential coastal marauder, the crow, including my own "Crow Vendetta Renga."

Dead Reckoning by Julie Burtinshaw (Vancouver, BC: Raincoast Books, 2001). A well-researched fictional account of the sinking of the steamship *Valencia* near Pachena Point in 1906. This tragedy in treacherous waters known as the Graveyard of the Pacific spurred Canadian federal authorities to build the seventy-seven-kilometre West Coast Trail and to build a chain of lighthouses along this particularly lethal stretch of the west Vancouver Island coastline. Written for teens, but as with all good writing, it's a book all ages will appreciate.

December Tide by Julia Moe (Madeira Park, BC: Harbour Publishing, 1978). A lovely first book of poems that linger and resonate by a long-time lightkeeper and, more recently, caretaker of the Bernt Ronning Garden near Holberg, BC, with husband and former lightkeeper Ron Moe.

The Light Between Oceans by M.L. Stedman (New York, NY: Scribner, 2013). Set in Australia after World War I, this novel is a wonderful evocation of early lighthouse life.

Lighthouse Island by Paulette Jiles (New York, NY: HarperCollins, 2013). The author spent a week on Lennard Island while researching this brilliant literary dystopian novel, and (toot, toot!) Jeff George's photograph of the Lennard Island Lighthouse is featured on the cover.

Moominpappa at Sea by Tove Jansson, translated by Kingsley Hart (New York, NY: Farrar, Straus and Giroux, 1993). Ostensibly for children, this whimsical Jansson classic captures the oppressive paranoia some people cannot shake when on a small island surrounded by heavy seas. It is worth reading by all ages for its astute observations about mental health and living in isolation.

The Sea Runners by Ivan Doig (New York, NY: Scribner, 1982, 2006). Based on the true story of the escape by sea of four indentured labourers from a Russian work camp in Alaska. An astonishing and well-written depiction of the rigours of long-distance sea travel by canoe.

The Shapes of Our Singing: A Comprehensive Guide to Verse Forms and Metres From Around the World by Robin Skelton (Spokane, WA: Eastern Washington University Press, 2002). My guide to writing Japanese form poems. It includes all the major and minor verse forms from around the world, over three hundred forms.

This Dark by Joanna Streetly, illustrated by Marion Syme (Tofino, BC: Postelsia Press, 2014). Perfect, profound haiku that explore the light and dark aspects of West Coast living by a poet, novelist, artist, kayak guide and long-time Clayoquot Sound float house resident. Includes gorgeous black-and-white linocuts by a Tofino artist and children's book illustrator.

U-Turn: What If You Woke Up One Morning and Realized You Were Living the Wrong Life? by Bruce Grierson (New York, NY: Bloomsbury, 2008). An exploration of when and why people drastically change the way they are living their lives. Read it, and then just do it.

TWO BC FILMS ABOUT LIGHTHOUSES

Beautiful Lennard Island by Beverly Shaffer (director), National Film Board of Canada, 1977 (23 min 45 sec). Steven Holland, the ten-year-old son of lightkeepers Tony and Margaret Holland, is the gracious host of this charming film about living on a lightstation with his mother, father and younger brother, David. (Steven is now an astrophysicist! Rumour has it that David has done well in real estate, foreshadowed in the film!)

Leaving the Lights by Chris Jaksa (director), National Film Board of Canada, 2004 (40 min). Ed and Pat Kidder, BC's longest-serving lightkeepers at the time, were awarded the Queen's Jubilee Medal for their stalwart service to the public, involving over 125 incidents with many lives saved due to their direct intervention. This documentary follows their last days at Nootka Lightstation as they are about to retire. It's funny and sad, too, as the Kidders deeply love Nootka, as do all of us who ever work at this very special lightstation.

INTERESTING WEBSITES

Canadian Lightkeepers Association: www.canadianlightkeepers.org. Canadian lightkeepers and their supporters helped to fund and form this website in 2010 to keep each other and the public aware of news stories involving acts of heroism by lightkeepers and other newsworthy stories pertaining to lighthouses.

Environment Canada's Weather and Meteorology page: www.ec.gc.ca/meteo-weather. Has a link to marine topics including instructions on how to make marine weather observations and information about Canada's marine warning program.

Lighthouse Memories: www.lighthousememories.ca. This excellent site has information about and photographs of all of the staffed and historic lightstations in BC. It is founded and maintained by former BC lightkeeper John Coldwell. I especially like this site because the scope is now truly international. If you are keen on "all things lighthouse-y," this is your go-to website with lots of good photos, frequent updates and a Facebook corner, as well as historical information.

Lighthouses of British Columbia: www.fogwhistle.ca/bclights. This site is also run by a former BC lightkeeper, Ron Ammundsen. It has an excellent map of currently staffed BC lightstations, photos and other interesting information.

Seeing the Light: Report on Staffed Lighthouses in Newfoundland and Labrador and British Columbia. Report of the Standing Senate Committee for the Department of Fisheries and Oceans, December 2010: www.parl.gc.ca/Content/SEN/Committee/403/fish/rep/repo6dec10-e.pdf